Sign with Your Baby

D1321923

Teach Yourself®

Sign with Your Baby

Jane Jarvis

For UK order enquiries: please contact Bookpoint Ltd,
130 Milton Park, Abingdon, Oxon OX14 4SB.
Telephone: +44 (0) 1235 827720. Fax: +44 (0) 1235 400454.
Lines are open 09.00–17.00, Monday to Saturday, with a 24-hour
message answering service. Details about our titles and how to
order are available at www.teachyourself.co.uk

Long renowned as the authoritative source for self-guided learning –
with more than 50 million copies sold worldwide – the **Teach Yourself**
series includes over 500 titles in the fields of languages, crafts, hobbies,
business, computing and education.

British Library Cataloguing in Publication Data: a catalogue record
for this title is available from the British Library.

First published in UK 2008 by Hodder Education, part of Hachette
UK, 338 Euston Road, London NW1 3BH.

This edition published 2010.

Previously published as *Teach Yourself Baby Signing*.

The **Teach Yourself** name is a registered trade mark of Hodder
Headline.

Typeset by MPS Limited, a Macmillan Company.

Printed in Great Britain for Hodder Education, an Hachette UK
Company, 338 Euston Road, London NW1 3BH, by CPI Cox &
Wyman, Reading, Berkshire RG1 8EX.

The publisher has used its best endeavours to ensure that the URLs
for external websites referred to in this book are correct and active
at the time of going to press. However, the publisher and the
author have no responsibility for the websites and can make no
guarantee that a site will remain live or that the content will remain
relevant, decent or appropriate.

Hachette UK's policy is to use papers that are natural, renewable
and recyclable products and made from wood grown in sustainable
forests. The logging and manufacturing processes are expected to
conform to the environmental regulations of the country of origin.

Impression number   10 9 8 7 6 5 4 3 2 1
Year   2014 2013 2012 2011 2010

Acknowledgements

I would like to take this opportunity to express my sincere, heartfelt thanks firstly to Sasha Felix, Director of Sing and Sign. Without her vision and leadership, Sing and Sign wouldn't be what it is today. Sasha not only inspired me to begin signing with my own children, but to begin teaching parents how to sign with their own babies. Later on I joined Sasha in the office, co-ordinating the local franchise area and liaising with the many franchisees, all of whom wanted to share the wonders of baby signing with other parents. My time with Sing and Sign was fantastic, and I truly miss them since my move to Australia.

I would also like to thank my wonderful husband for giving me the space to write this book and taking on extra childcare duties (and I *so* wanted to say extra cleaning duties too – but, hey, you can't have it all!). This book began while I was working within the Sing and Sign family in the UK, but finished when there was just the four of us, following a huge international move. We thought that hectic writing time was over, but then there was a book relaunch with a young baby added to the mix. Juggling work, children, home education, church life, sleepless nights and the usual 'life' stuff has been interesting! Team Jarvis has certainly pulled through again, but your love and support during this time has been invaluable.

This book also wouldn't have been possible without the support of my parents and my in-laws, who at different times have either offered me the quietness of their house or helped with childcare to enable me to finish this project – a huge THANK YOU to you.

This book wouldn't be complete without fantastic parents who have been passionate about signing with their children and wanted to share their story. Thank you to all who contributed, whether your story made it to final publication or not.

This book was also helped by my wonderful friends who proofread, gave expert medical advice and general help and encouragement. Most of you asked not to be named – but you know who you are – and I appreciate you all!

Contents

Meet the author

Welcome to *Sign with Your Baby*!

My interest in signing and specifically baby signing began long before I had children. I saw a segment on the television which I found fascinating and resolved that when the time came I would look into the subject further. I now have three beautiful children aged eight, six and six months who vary vastly in many ways. The two older ones were poles apart in their signing and speech and language development and we've had some special needs to consider along the way. I'm about to start my signing time all over again, but in reality I haven't actually stopped! I regularly, subtly and without words remind my older boys to say please and thank you when they forget. If they are engrossed in some play activity and are jigging up and down, I quickly use the signs 'toilet' and 'now'. With my younger son, who is still in the early reading phase, I will often use signs to help with his reading or when we are singing to help him when he can't read the words.

I was born, raised and have spent most of my life along the south coast of England. Living on the outskirts of Brighton – a large, vibrant and diverse city, with a cosmopolitan, multicultural, alternative theme running through its veins – we were spoilt when it came to everything baby. We could, if we so desired, enrol for yoga, golf or Spanish, and there were music classes aplenty. It was the Sing and Sign music classes that drew my eye and reminded me of the television segment years earlier. At almost seven months, and having spent much of his early life in and out of hospital, my son was enrolled in his first class. Within weeks he was signing, and quickly became very proficient. I was amazed at what a difference signing made to his little life, how it lessened his frustration and enabled him to communicate so far beyond the level of his peers and, indeed, my expectations. During those first couple of years, especially the non-verbal months, signing was a lifesaver for us. When he was really sick he could let me know which part of his body was experiencing pain. To begin with, I was slightly clueless as to how much a young non-verbal baby understood, however, I soon realized that a baby's understanding far supersedes their early ability to communicate. Signing helped us through many struggles, and gave us many laughs, too. It enabled me to easily enter his world, going beyond knowing his basic needs for love, food and sleep, and avoiding tantrums from not being understood. It gave him a way to express himself to me.

Such was my passion for signing, I was soon asked if I would like to train to become a teacher. I loved inspiring other parents to sign with their babies and reap the many benefits associated with it. As I moved into a more administrative role within Sing and Sign, I co-ordinated the local classes and had the opportunity to speak with even more parents about the wonders of communicating with your pre-verbal baby. This enthusiasm for inspiring others led me to speak on television and radio about the benefits of baby signing.

Early in 2007 we made a mighty move across the continents to the western coast of Australia. Baby signing is not so well known here, and is associated with the deaf community rather than being seen as a way for hearing babies to communicate before speech develops. In the few years I've been here, however, I can already see this perception slowly beginning to change and I hope that one day I will go back to teaching and spreading the message about the benefits of baby signing. For now, though, I am at the point of introducing my baby to the joys of what simple songs and gestures can really communicate.

Only got a minute?

Baby signing is a wonderful way to unlock your baby's world – an opportunity to get to know your child's thoughts, desires and needs on a deeper level and at a much earlier age than you thought possible. Baby signing is so natural that many of us are already 'signing' without realizing it. The first, most obvious sign that most parents use with their baby is a wave goodbye. We say the word and teach the sign at every opportunity. It is amazing how quickly our babies respond, understand, *and* use the sign in context. Baby signing is a natural extension of this, giving further intentional signs for themes or items your baby is particularly interested in. The theme of animals dominates a baby's world, and many boys are interested in anything that moves, so giving them signs for bikes, cars, trains and so on can be inspiring for them. So, in essence, baby signing is using simple signs or hand gestures for important and relevant words in your baby's world.

Below are some first signs to begin with.

MILK

The same sign can be used for 'milk' whether you are breast- or bottle-feeding. *Make a fist, then open and close your fist as if you are milking a cow. Say the word 'milk'.*

ALL GONE/FINISHED

This is a versatile sign to use many times throughout the day: when you have finished feeding, your peek-a-boo game is over or a visitor leaves the house. *Begin by holding your fists together with your palms facing inwards, then move your hands out so your hands are flat and facing down. Say 'all gone'.*

Milk.

All gone.

5 Only got five minutes?

The two essential keys to successful baby signing are:

▶ *keeping it simple*
▶ *focusing on learning gestures/signs for the things your baby enjoys and is most inspired by.*

Learning to speak the English language is a complex journey for a young child. Children need to be and are usually readily exposed to language – the ebb and flow, intonations, the lilt of your voice. However, babies understand at a mono-word level. Recognizing this important fact enables us to adjust and simplify our speech. For example, you may be commenting to your baby, 'Look at the big, brown dog – can you see him running after the ball?' Your baby may delight in hearing the sound of your voice, but may not understand your sentence. A more meaningful exchange for a baby might include the following changes.

'Look at the *dog*' (emphasizing and signing the word dog). 'The *dog* is running after the ball.' Your baby's attention will naturally be drawn to the word 'dog', not only because of the visual clue of seeing the dog, but also as a result of your providing the word and sign to match. Simplifying sentences for your pre-verbal baby will naturally slow down your speech and enable your child to understand and begin to try and say the word 'dog'. Once she has grasped these initial words (usually nouns), it is time to add the further building blocks of language by introducing adjectives and eventually getting back to the original '*big, brown* dog'.

Add to your baby's own repertoire of gestures (she may wave hello or hold her arms up to be picked up) by adding some further intentional signs – such as those for food, or a drink or for changing a nappy (see below). Use signs that relate to your daily routines with your baby, such as going out, or signs for bath and bed. Try to notice themes or items in which your baby is particularly interested.

EAT

Bunch your fingertips together and gently tap the corner of your mouth as you emphasize saying the word 'eat'.

DRINK

Shape your hand as if you were holding a beaker, lift it a few times to your mouth, and say the word 'drink'.

10 Only got ten minutes?

Some people are unsure of starting to sign with their baby as they believe the myth that baby signing might in some way inhibit a baby's natural instinct to learn to talk. You can be reassured that this is certainly not the case. Studies dating back as far as Werner and Kaplan in the early 1960s, right up to the present day, show that the opposite is actually true. When signing with your baby it is vital to *always* say the word as you sign it. The sign is supporting the spoken word and not replacing it. The introduction of baby signing will inspire a baby to develop enhanced communication skills and will greatly develop his language skills. Children become far better communicators when their early attempts at communication are understood and meet a response.

Dr Marilyn Daniels says:

> *Including sign language in the communication mix can eliminate the frustration both parent and child often experience as they attempt to comprehend one another. It fosters pleasant discourse, clarifies meaning and creates better understanding between them. With keener understanding, there also comes an authentic grasp of content. Sign does not hinder language development in any way, rather it fosters it. It picks up on the natural visual acuity young children possess and uses it to the child's advantage.*

The benefits of baby signing are significant for both parent and child, with some benefits for the child continuing long after he is out of baby- and toddlerhood. So, let's take a closer look at some of the research supporting the advantages of signing with your baby.

The most significant research into baby signing began in the early 1980s, when a ground-breaking 20-year study was undertaken, comparing the impact of signing with the development of babies who did not sign. The study was devised to look at how baby signing affected children's linguistic and intellectual development. They were able to identify the progress of the children at two, three and eight years old. Their results were amazing and made compelling reading.

The main conclusions this study arrived at were that babies who themselves signed, or who were shown signs:

▶ *consistently achieved higher results than their peers*
▶ *spoke in sentences earlier*
▶ *at age three had language skills of children a year older*
▶ *by age eight had scored significantly higher in IQ tests.*

The research concluded that using baby signs improves language and cognitive ability, and that the advantages did not end when babies began to speak. Baby signing has far reaching implications long after the child has stopped using the signs.

The very latest research in the United States (early 2009) has revealed that 'young children who pick up gestures and signs from their parents by 14 months have larger and more complex vocabularies when they start school'. The primary reason for this is that by learning to point and use signs, children become better at connecting words to objects. The signs/gesture effect may also have a lasting influence on children's intellectual development because a child's vocabulary at the start of school is known to be a strong predictor of later academic success.

Other benefits of baby signing:

▶ *parents speak more slowly – thinking about their child's understanding at a one-word level – so their baby can focus on what they are saying*
▶ *enhanced early vocabulary and understanding*
▶ *parents focus on their baby's needs, thought process and interests*

- *enhanced eye contact and shared looking*
- *communication that would otherwise not be possible, with the opportunity to explore complex ideas earlier*
- *encourages a greater level of trust between parent and child – the baby knows that the parent understands what is being communicated*
- *an above average ability later on to learn a new language*
- *reduced frustration levels*
- *the ability to give meaning to more abstract words or concepts.*

Research clearly indicates that gesture is a very natural part of language development and aids the developing communication skills of your child. Communication through speech is the essence of being human, but using additional specific and intentional gestures (or signs) can improve language skills and help babies both with understanding and talking. However, it is important not to lose sight, amid the excellent research and evidence of benefits, of the opportunity to provide both parents and babies with a rich, rewarding first experience of communication, which helps to develop a deeper bond between parent and child.

Introduction

This book will teach you how to:

▶ *understand the principles of baby signing*
▶ *know the benefits of signing with your baby*
▶ *begin signing with your baby*
▶ *introduce signs that are relevant to your baby's world*
▶ *be aware of any special needs and what action to take*
▶ *continue using appropriate signs with older children.*

People have been signing with their babies for years; in fact, it is so natural that most of us already use signs and gestures with our babies without realizing it! The most common reason for doing so is an intense desire on the part of a parent to find out exactly what is going on in a baby's mind – what do they need? What does she want? What does she think about and remember? All parents want what is best for their children, and one of the fundamental ways to nurture and understand a child is by good communication.

Babies often have more intelligence than we give them credit for, purely because they have limited means to let us know what their thoughts and needs are. Their undeveloped vocal cords restrict them from fully participating in the verbal language around them, and in fact most babies' vocal cords must develop for 16 months or so before they can pronounce clear words. However, the good news is that babies develop the fine muscles in their hands long before they develop those muscles required for speech, so they're equipped to communicate with you long before they can speak. Baby signing can help parents, carers and all of those important people in a child's world to understand them, interact with them, and most importantly to have lots of fun.

This book aims not only to inspire and help you to introduce signing with your child, it also shows you many practical signs that are useful for you and your baby. You will find references and illustrations to over 100 signs within the book, and many more on the accompanying CD-ROM.

Please note that the male and female pronouns have been alternated in each chapter of the book. This is for convenience only and not because the chapters are gender-specific.

1

··

History and principles of baby signing

In this chapter you will learn:
- *what baby signing is and how it all began*
- *how signing is beneficial to your baby's development*
- *the Sing and Sign approach to baby signing.*

Early communication

To understand baby signing, it can be helpful to go back and think through the earliest forms of communication we can have with our baby.

Even from within the womb, babies are trying to communicate. You may be surprised to discover parents have recorded 'communicating' or 'playing' with their unborn babies in the womb. By pressing or rubbing one side of the mother's stomach, an unborn baby may respond to the touch with a kick or an elbow; by repeating it on the other side, parents can 'play' and communicate with their unborn baby. Babies also respond to loud music and even their parents' singing. All of these are the earliest forms of communication. The awareness of speech sounds is also developing during this time in the womb. Researchers have discovered that an unborn baby's heart rate will increase at the sound of his mother's voice. Having continual communication is important for babies and children. By reading stories, singing and talking to your baby, even in the womb, parents can help to promote developing language skills.

From birth until about four months of age, babies' principal communication consists mainly of reflexive crying to express feelings of hunger, tiredness, boredom or pain. Much of their communication will be through facial expressions and the movements of their arms, legs and fingers. They will also use smiling, cooing and other sounds of pleasure to communicate needs and feelings. Mirroring sounds and early words, responding to their communication as well as answering your baby's cries are all ways to start your baby on the road to speech.

Liz Attenborough, manager of the Talk To Your Baby campaign, said:

The level of interaction between young children and adults has a significant impact on their communication skills later in life.

Studies on Romanian orphans who received little contact with adults in their early life have found that they have language problems for the rest of their lives.

Babies are born without all their neurological pathways connected, so their interactions during the first few months and years of life play an important part in how they develop.

The next stage of communication is what has been referred to as 'babbling'. At the age of around four to six months, babies start to make many more sounds, including vowel sounds. Before speaking words, babies practise the sounds, intonations and rhythms of language, as well as extensive body language and facial expressions to communicate. Interestingly, babies will often babble more when they are alone. Through interaction with you, babies mirror and learn early language skills. Many parents will find they adjust their speech and use 'motherease' or 'baby talk', trying hard to interpret unintelligible utterances! This helps to socialize children with simplified language and introduces them gradually to adult language.

Between six and 12 months, most babies are beginning to use a combination of gestures and sounds to make themselves understood. This is a charming but very frustrating stage of their development. From around six months, babies begin to reach for objects: babies love 'peek-a-boo' and will show willingness to continue the game on and on, by reaching towards your hand or whatever you are using to hide behind. Words begin to have some meaning but this will be very context dependent. During this time, babies begin to respond to some simple requests such as 'up you come'. At around nine months, communication becomes increasingly intentional: your baby may give or show an object as a way to communicate, which paves the way for pointing. He may begin to understand names of familiar objects and people. His babbling may begin to be produced in longer strings ('bababa mamama'). Your baby will often point at things, shake his head for 'no' and wave. These are symbolic gestures that are one form of communication used by pre-verbal babies and toddlers.

In addition to pointing and grunting, and trying to 'sing' to music, your baby has the potential use of his hands and body to aid in communicating thoughts, wants, fears, needs and memories. At this point, they are beginning to understand a lot about themselves and their world, but most babies are still lacking a precise way to express their thoughts and needs.

The first single words (usually a child's version of the adult word, e.g. 'du' for 'duck') tend to be spoken at around 12 months. At around this time, you will notice that your baby understands the names of people and objects if they are in their usual context. At this stage, babies often use lots of gestures to express meaning, as their understanding is typically in advance of actual spoken language. They will often invent 'signs' to convey their meaning (arms to be lifted up, etc.).

By around 14–20 months of age, children will usually begin to combine gestures with actual words. They begin with simple words that they will have heard often, such as 'mama' or 'dada'. These words eventually turn into two-word phrases, which is the next step on the journey of speech. Two-word phrases, such as 'shoes on', 'doggie gone', or 'Daddy home', begin around the age of two years. However, in your baby's fast developing world, this is a very long time to wait to be fully understood. Using signs and gestures gives babies a way to effectively 'talk' with their parents, long before they can use speech to communicate. It is more effective and precise than cooing, crying, smiling, grunting or flapping their hands, and eliminates much of the guesswork associated with a young child. Babies can, and do, communicate about the world around them long before they have mastered their verbal speaking skills.

Please note: The ages given are merely a guide – it's important to note that, like other aspects of development, the process of acquiring language is gradual and varies greatly between children.

What *is* baby signing?

Baby signing is really very easy and doesn't need too much explanation. It is, in essence, simple hand gestures. Signing is so natural that you are probably already 'signing' to your baby without realizing it! Most of us will wave goodbye to babies happily and comfortably all the time without even thinking much about it. We all know this helps them start to understand what 'goodbye' means, and that when they wave back to us they are well on their way to saying 'bye-bye' too. This is, in reality, a baby's first 'sign'.

Throughout this book you will find many examples and case studies of parents signing with their children to give you confidence and inspire you in your own baby-signing journey. Parents have often said how helpful it is to hear other stories, not only as encouragement, but also to suggest creative ways of using signing that they may not have thought of.

Most children will point, wave and nod and shake their heads. Baby signing classes, and this book, aim to help and encourage parents to use a few more gestures or 'signs' for other important and relevant words in your baby's world. It isn't necessary to learn a whole dictionary of sign language.

Insight

The key to inspiring your own baby's signing is to pick a few gestures for the things your baby is most inspired by and enjoys.

Baby signing will help you to help your baby understand sooner, and effectively communicate with you earlier and more successfully during the long process of learning to talk!

Parents can sometimes think signing with their baby is harder and more complicated than it is, not realizing that it is an extension of natural communication.

I had no idea how easy signing was with your baby – I was a little sceptical at first. We learnt many of the signs through songs – which really helped. Also a lot of the signs mimic an activity or movement, or represent a shape of an object so they are easily remembered. The wider family have been communicating easily and effectively with my son, and the difference is amazing.

Martin, dad of Josiah

How baby signing began

Although sign language itself has records dating as far back as the 16th century, significant interest in baby sign language began in the early 1980s, when two separate and convincing research projects took place. One project was undertaken by Joseph Garcia – a student at Alaska Pacific University – and a ground-breaking

20-year study was undertaken by pioneers in the field:
Linda Acredolo, Ph.D and Susan Goodwyn, Ph.D, both from
the University of California, Davis. These two research projects
were inspired by the researchers' own children.

As baby signing is still an emerging phenomenon, especially within
the UK, it is important to document all of the research in this
area. It is also helpful to understand some of the roots of baby
signing. However, if you are really keen to move straight onto the
mechanics and practical instruction on how to begin signing with
your baby, then you may wish to move directly to Chapter 2, and
come back to read this section later.

During the 1970s, Garcia worked as an interpreter and became
fascinated with his observations that babies of his deaf friends were
becoming sign language 'experts' around the age of nine months.
In the same way, his studies also showed that babies of hearing
parents were not communicating much at this same point in their
development. In 1987, while attending Alaska Pacific University,
Garcia began to research the use of American Sign Language (ASL)
for hearing babies of hearing parents, and the effect this would
have on their communication.

Garcia's own infant sons were a great advantage in his research,
and became 'test subjects' for what eventually developed into his
'Sign With Your Baby' and 'Sign 2 Me' programmes based on
American Sign Language.

At around the same time, Linda Acredolo had observed her
daughter, Katie, watching the fish swimming in the fish tank at the
paediatrician's office. Katie walked up to the tank to take a closer
look and started to blow. Her mother was puzzled at her daughter's
behaviour. Once they were home, Katie was put down for a nap in
her cot. Above the cot hung a beautiful fish mobile, which Acredolo
set in motion with a gentle blow. It was at that point she remembered
her daughter in the paediatrician's office and immediately made the
connection of Katie 'communicating' with the fish earlier that day.

Over two decades, Acredolo, her research partner, Goodwyn, and their team began to study the impact of signing with babies as compared to those babies who did not sign. They were funded by a grant from the US National Institute of Child Health and Human Development and they were able to identify the progress of children at two, three and eight years old.

This amazing 20-year study was devised to look at 'how baby signing affected children's linguistic and intellectual development'. The study began by comparing three groups of 11-month-old babies:

Group One: Parents were asked to encourage baby signing (alongside speech) when interacting.

Group Two: Parents were to focus on naming things (verbally) for their baby.

Group Three: Parents had no specific instruction at all.

The babies underwent a language assessment at regular intervals up to the age of three and were followed up again at age eight. Their initial results were amazing and made compelling reading. The tests showed that the baby signers' language skills (Group One) were in advance of the non-signers and that they spoke in sentences earlier. At three years of age, the baby signers had language skills normally expected of four-year-olds. At age eight, the children who had used baby signs scored significantly higher on the IQ test than the non-signers.

Acredolo and Goodwyn continued with their research and provided psychology scholars with interesting results. Two decades of research results proved signers out-performed non-signers in many areas of cognition and language development. They concluded that using baby signs improves language and cognitive ability and, furthermore, that this did not end when babies started to talk, and that in fact using baby signing has far-reaching implications long after the child has stopped using the signs.

The results of Acredolo and Goodwyn's work formed the basis of their book and programme, *Baby Signs*. The book is based on a concept that allows babies to create their own signs to communicate in order to bridge the gap between cognition and communication. They primarily recommend that parents invent signs to use with their babies, not necessarily following any formal system. This approach can be valuable as parents are inspired to be constantly on the lookout for things their baby is interested in and to invent signs accordingly, which would be relevant to their child's own interests. However, a parent would have to be highly motivated and resourceful to invent, remember and stick to a set of signs they themselves have created and which no one else understands.

From this significant research study and the resulting sign language programmes, many grass roots baby sign-language programmes have emerged from America. Many of the current programmes are based on American Sign Language (ASL) and have verbal development as their goal. Without the statistical research from Acredolo and Goodwyn, we may not be aware of the positive impact that the introduction of sign language has on a baby's cognitive and language development.

The research shows that gesture is a natural part of the development of language and communication skills. Communication through speech is the essence of being human; it's what distinguishes us from the animal world. Using extra specific gestures (or baby signs) can improve language skills and help babies both with understanding and talking as well as providing both parents and babies with a rich, rewarding first experience of communication.

My interest in baby signing was raised by a friend who described watching a family signing together. As someone who uses BSL (British Sign Language), she approached the family to ask more about the child who was signing. They explained that they were using baby sign language and how useful it had been. They described how it helped ease

The benefits of baby signing

The rewards of signing with your baby are potentially very significant. As we have already discovered in the section on the history of baby signing, research has shown us many of the benefits of signing with your baby. However, there is still interesting ongoing research into the effect of baby signing on the development of a baby's brain. In the earliest years of life, babies' brains are 'wiring' themselves through their experiences. While using signs, parents say accompanying words and tend to give increased language input, giving their child the opportunity of a greater understanding of words and concepts. For example, you may see a cat and say to your baby, 'Do you see the *cat*? Look he's high up there in the tree. He's a lovely big, black *cat*. I wonder how high he can climb?' etc. Instinctively you have talked about something that is of interest, given more information, and very naturally enhanced the word 'cat'. Your baby hears more spoken words, and different ideas and concepts in a very natural and relaxed way.

Signing has allowed us to understand each other from very early on; I feel that he started telling me what interests him, what he does and doesn't want to do and what's going on in 'his world' months before he was able to talk. I'm sure our ability to communicate through signs has not only strengthened our bond, but also helps us avoid too many tantrums!

Jane Kirkby with her son Ben

Signing babies can communicate complex things earlier. Many experts suggest this stimulates brain development and enhances the building of brain circuitry.

In her fascinating book, *Dancing With Words, Signing for Hearing Children's Literacy*, Professor Marilyn Daniels of Pennsylvania State University writes:

Sign language instruction, with its requisite visual component, creates an increase in brain activity by engaging the visual cortex and presenting an additional language to the young learner. The heightened cerebral action occurs in both the right and left hemispheres of the brain. This increase in language activity stimulates the development of the brain by stimulating the formation of more synapses, or connections among brain cells. The brains of children up to about the age of eight continue to develop and grow in this manner in response to environmental input. Brain cells literally live or die as language experiences impinge upon them. Using sign language and English in tandem provides a much richer language base for brain activity and brain growth and development.

Professor Daniels also likens signing to 'making pictures in the air' – an incredibly useful tool when trying to give meaning to words that are abstract or concepts that are difficult for your baby to understand. You may find telling your child to put his coat on because it is cold outside, or his hat on because it is windy, are actually difficult concepts for him to understand, as he can't see the cold or the wind. A bag of frozen peas can help illustrate the 'cold' sign, and you may find it then becomes one they use quite quickly!

Insight
Using signs and gestures – making words visual – can often make a difficult concept easily understood by your baby.

'Signing' has been a brilliant asset for us as Rosie has been able to avoid the whole phase of frustration that comes before they can talk. The signing started to come out just as Rosie got seriously ill for the first time with chickenpox and she was able to tell me

As we have already covered many of the benefits of signing with your baby, here are just a few edited highlights.

Baby signing allows babies to enjoy:

- *communication that would otherwise not be possible*
- *enhanced early vocabulary and understanding*
- *increased confidence from being more readily understood*
- *greater than average ability later on in life to learn a new language*
- *reduced frustration levels (for parent and baby).*

Baby signing helps parents to:

- *stimulate their baby's intellectual and emotional development*
- *enrich their baby's relationships*
- *share a deeper bond with their baby because they have greater insight into his mind, thoughts, needs and ideas*
- *obtain a higher level of trust from their baby because he knows that they understand what he is trying to tell them*
- *gain satisfaction from the knowledge that you can effectively communicate with your pre-verbal infant*
- *encourage the development of speech.*

So, what about British baby signing?

Across the UK, there are now many signing programmes available to parents. However, after much research and for the purposes of this book, we are focusing on the Sing and Sign approach to baby signing.

Sing and Sign was the first British baby-signing programme and its original and unique approach has revolutionized baby signing in the UK. The programme was devised by mother and musician Sasha Felix, and developed with the help of speech and language professionals, launching in January 2001. The programme began with local classes, but such was the interest that a DVD was launched later on that year which has since taught thousands of parents across the world how to sign with their babies and encourage early communication.

Within three years of its launch, Sing and Sign was being recommended by Sure Start, the government-backed service working to promote all aspects of development in babies and young children.

Sing and Sign is a brilliant programme. We suggest all our mums and babies use signs, as gesture is a natural first form of communication. The gestures shown in Sing and Sign can help babies understand more of what is said to them and enables babies to express themselves earlier. Using signs can make life for parents far less stressful!

Susan Duffy, Speech and Language Therapist for Sure Start

With such positive research initially coming through from the United States, and the myths (see Chapter 8) surrounding teaching babies how to sign before speech slowly being eradicated, the press soon took hold of the baby signing phenomenon and it wasn't long before many other baby signing programmes began to develop – especially within the UK. Some began as evening classes teaching parents and adults basic signs to use with their babies, others taught British Sign Language (see Chapter 8), while many others took place in a parent-and-child setting and focused primarily on signing with your own child.

It would be impossible to cover adequately every baby-signing programme that is currently available to parents within the UK and for that reason, this book concentrates on just one programme that will hopefully help, encourage and inspire you and therefore be the most beneficial way forward on your own baby-signing journey. The last part of this chapter will outline the Sing and Sign approach to baby signing, which will help you understand the methodology behind the teaching in the rest of the book.

The Sing and Sign approach to teaching baby signing

Everyone knows that babies and children enjoy nursery rhymes and action songs, and that musical activities help to stimulate language development. In slightly older children, doing things rhythmically begins to get children moving in a way that persuasion and even bribery cannot. Sing and Sign is unique in the fact that it so effectively combines the benefits of both music and baby signing.

The research literature on music enrichment for infants and toddlers has been prolific. We know that music participation teaches music skills, perception, and cognition. Simultaneously it also promotes child development areas such as listening skills, language development, motor coordination, cooperative social skills and reciprocity ... demonstrating the power of music to be a highly beneficial reinforcer for children from the moment of their birth.

Jayne Standley, Ph.D

The aim of the Sing and Sign approach is for babies to enjoy the musical and social aspect of classes while their parents learn about baby signing. The programme aims to tap into the highly gestural phase of a baby's life and, using a thorough and well-developed format, take them right through until they are mastering speech.

Insight

Part of the pleasure of baby signing for parents can be the friendships that grow with other baby-signing families. It is so wonderful to see young babies communicating with each other, and being understood.

Sing and Sign teaches a wide range of signs using some traditional and some specially written or adapted songs in a fun and relaxed way. What makes the programme special is that every sign used in a song relates to those important first words of a baby's world: nappies and bathtime; hiding games and bedtime; going to the park, and other things that capture a child's imagination such as animals and vehicles. You name it, the programme has a song about it, and the babies just love to hear them!

Sign with Your Baby aims to follow the curriculum of the course – as much as is possible within the confines of a book. We will use the same guidelines that are presented in class, as well as following some of the order and routines of topics that you will find on the course. These can be found primarily in Chapters 2, 3 and 4. The course is full of songs and rhymes, whereas this book is only able to offer a few ideas to enable you to sing your way through routines.

I took Natasha and her older sister out in the car. In my mirror I saw her signing the beginning of the song 'Wind the bobbin up', so we ended up singing it to her about 30 times – she was very happy!

Melanie Warren

The curriculum is designed with the aim not only to give you, the parent, continuity with learning the signs, but to give the added aspect of routine for the babies – and we know how much babies love routine. On the course, songs, puppets, props, pictures and instruments are used to help inspire your baby's interest and facilitate in illustrating the signs. Using this book at home you can be inventive with how to present the signs to your baby. Throughout this book you will also find many examples of straightforward ways in which to introduce the signs to your baby, as well as integrating them into your daily living. The signs are separated into basic signs and secondary signs.

BASIC SIGNS

These signs are appropriate to all babies and cover familiar daily routines. Parents are first encouraged to use the routine basic signs with confidence, introducing more on a weekly basis. In class, particular basic signs are highlighted as 'Signs of the Week' for parents to begin using at home. By participating in Sing and Sign groups at Stage One, parents become familiar with more than 80 basic signs. Alongside this instruction, parents are also shown many potentially motivating secondary signs.

SECONDARY SIGNS

These signs cover animals, vehicles, toys, etc. and, although shown in class, are more usually used away from class and when baby is ready. From the wide variety of secondary signs covered in Sing and Sign Stage One, parents can use those which best suit their baby's interests. Once a baby begins to communicate interest in things by pointing, then more secondary signs can be shown.

You will find both basic and secondary signs are covered within this book, enabling you to show your child a wide variety of signs to help stimulate their interest and encourage communication.

We started signing with Tahlia when she was seven months old, using a book. We've been taking her to Sing and Sign classes since she was nine months old and they've become her favourite activity of the week. She kicks her legs with

(Contd)

All the songs are signed, but don't worry, there aren't so many
signs within the songs that you feel overwhelmed, just enough to
highlight the key words. Many of the tunes used are traditional
and familiar melodies, which ensures all songs are easy to sign
along with for the beginner. Within this book we have used only
the most traditional tunes with adjusted lyrics to enable you to
incorporate signing and singing easily into your daily routine.

Sing and Sign is a simple format that grows with your child.
Stage One is for babies of around six to seven months of age
and focuses on the basic and some secondary signs. Stage Two
is aimed at babies/toddlers aged around 14 months plus and,
again, the programme is ideal for their stage of development,
taking in concepts such as foods, weather and opposites, as well
as enjoying topics such as colours, basic counting and phonics.
By this time, many older babies are starting to use some words as
well as continuing to sign more difficult words. *Sign with Your
Baby* encompasses topics from both Stage One and Two of the
curriculum, covering signs that will be beneficial for the pre-verbal
baby, and those with emerging speech. We would recommend,
whatever the age of your child, starting at Chapter 2, which uses
the basic signs, and following through Chapter 3, 4 and 5.

The signs shown in Chapter 7 are more appropriate for babies aged
14 months plus, focusing on the older child, using more difficult
concepts and the use of phonics. If your child is experiencing any
developmental delay or problems with hearing or speech, then
Chapter 6 will be particularly important as it illustrates many of
the more common difficulties and special needs associated with
poor or delayed communication.

As the content and programme of Sing and Sign has been proved
to be so effective, during the course of this book we will be using
some of the material and signs used with kind permission of
Sasha Felix, Founder and Director of Sing and Sign.

10 THINGS TO REMEMBER

1   *Babies begin communicating in the womb, and move on to develop language skills (more complete sentences) usually between two-and-a-half and three-and-a-half years of age.*

2   *Babies can begin to show or tell you their wants and needs through signing from as young as six months.*

3   *Signing is a natural, easy way to communicate with your baby. Most parents use gestures naturally (such as waving goodbye), and baby signing is a way to expand on this, giving a few more intentional gestures.*

4   *Learning some intentional signs will help you to help your baby understand more quickly, and effectively communicate with you earlier and more successfully during the long process of learning to talk.*

5   *Studies have shown that baby signing improves language and cognitive ability. This extends beyond learning to talk and has far-reaching implications long after your child has stopped signing.*

6   *Baby signing gives meanings to abstract words or concepts that your child might otherwise have difficulty understanding.*

7   *Children who have learnt to sign before speech have an above-average ability to learn a new language later in life.*

8   *Babies who sign show less frustration than their peers and have enhanced early vocabulary and understanding.*

9   *Signing does not inhibit a baby's natural instinct to talk, in fact it encourages the development of speech.*

10 *Signing with your baby is beneficial for baby and parent – providing you both with a rich, rewarding first experience of communication.*

2

The early basics, getting started and basic guidelines

In this chapter you will learn:
- *when it is appropriate to start signing with your baby*
- *how to begin signing and identifying your baby's signs*
- *recommended initial signs to begin using with your baby.*

When should I start signing with my baby?

From around six to seven months is a great age to start using some simple key signs with your baby as this is when children become increasingly receptive to language. Starting earlier than this certainly won't harm your baby, but is usually more beneficial to the parent by allowing signing to become part of their daily life. However, it is important to note that by starting too early some parents may get discouraged and give up if their baby doesn't respond or takes a while to begin signing. Once a baby is six or seven months old, it is actually very easy to encourage and expand her natural communication into the use of sign language on a daily basis. It is usually at home, in context, that your baby will begin to understand and use the basic signs you have shown her, such as those for bathtime or bedtime.

Another, much less scientific, but also valid reason for starting at six months plus is because this is the age when your baby is often able, or learning, to sit up unaided (albeit with cushions around them). The benefit of this is threefold: not only does it gives you more freedom to face your baby and sustain eye contact with her, you have the freedom to use your hands to sign to her, and in addition, your baby, after accomplishing the epic task of learning to sit up, may well be more able to focus on learning additional skills. Signing is also more manageable for your baby once she is sitting up – it is a great skill to master and so difficult if you are lying on your back, and virtually impossible if you are lying or crawling on your front!

Insight

Parents' signing experience can vary considerably and can also vary from child to child. My first experience with signing was at a class with my first child who was about six-and-a-half months old. Within a few weeks he began signing 'milk', and quickly progressed, becoming an avid signer. My second child arrived 18 months later, so signing was already part of our lives, and we just continued. He signed his first sign around five and a half months (which is very early!) but he rarely signed until he was about 14 months of age, despite the fact that I was diligently and consistently signing to him. I do wonder if he had been my first child whether I would have given up, but having such a positive first experience ensured I continued. I was so glad I persisted. By 15 months he had a 'signing explosion' and became much more expressive – he really wanted to let us know by then what was going on in his little world. My six-month-old little girl is currently fascinated by the wiggling of my hands and fingers. One sign we use all the time at the moment is the 'open' sign. Every time she wakes from her nap, we go straight to the window and 'open' the blinds and we use it to 'open' her bag of toys. She uses the same intonation in her voice when I say 'open' – already it is clear how the word and the sign are giving clear meaning to her.

I started attending classes when my son was around six-and-a-half months. Within a couple of weeks he had signed his first sign, 'milk'. We were amazed, and very excited! He would often have his milk after dinner, but I had been busy and forgotten to give it to him. He took it upon himself to remind me. I was amazed that not only could he communicate his needs at such a young age, but it was totally in context and entirely appropriate.

Jane, mum of Jayden

However, if your baby is already older than six or seven months, don't worry – it's never too late to start signing with your baby. Maybe your baby is not yet talking, or maybe she only has a few words. Perhaps you have a toddler with an increasing vocabulary. In these cases, do start signing right away, focusing on what she is interested in. You can only enhance your communication with your child, have some fun and reap the many benefits of signing.

Insight

You may well discover that as your child is a little older, she is ready to begin telling you about her world straightaway, so use this opportunity to show her as many signs as possible.

Callum started attending signing classes at 16 months old and it has been a most rewarding experience. We both enjoy the classes and use the support material at home.

He is now 22 months old and although not yet talking, he communicates his needs perfectly. His first sign was for his bottle of milk and as our extended family uses most of the signs, now everyone knows what he wants.

(Contd)

We use Sing and Sign to complete everyday tasks in a fun way, using the 'Change your Nappy' song helps at changing times and the 'Where is it?' sign finds lost toys and clothes!

My friends who haven't discovered Sing and Sign are amazed at the signs Callum can make and at the level of communication and understanding we have – without a doubt Sing and Sign has enhanced our lives.

Vanessa

Guidelines for successful signing

Babies are all unique and you are the ideal judge of what signs will suit your baby best. However, a few simple guidelines will help you along the way. There are plenty of courses and approaches available – Sing and Sign is one of the most popular and has worked for many parents and children, which is the reason why we have used their guidelines and principles. Just remember to be consistent with your baby, don't give up and have fun!

TEN BASIC GUIDELINES FOR SUCCESSFUL BABY SIGNING

Follow these and you can't go wrong!

1 *Begin with basics such as 'eat', 'drink', 'milk', 'more' and 'all gone' (finished).*
2 *Follow your baby's lead.*
3 *Always say the word as you sign.*
4 *Speak slowly but naturally.*
5 *Keep it simple.*
6 *Happily accept any signing attempts by your baby.*
7 *Be consistent.*
8 *Avoid trying to get your baby to 'perform' signs.*
9 *Be patient and relaxed about baby signing.*
10 *Praise, praise, praise!*

When will my baby start to sign?

Signing comes more quickly for some babies than others, just as speech or walking does. Babies are all gloriously different in the speed and nature of various aspects of their development. From around six to eight months of age, children become increasingly receptive to language, which is why we recommend showing some key signs from this age. Your baby will start to use the signs you show her when she is ready and has something to say.

Insight

In my experience it is very difficult to predict when a child will begin to sign. Some parents admit they haven't been very consistent with showing their child signs, and yet their child begins to sign anyway. Others, like myself, may be very consistent in signing, but in the case of my second child he only showed me a few signs between the ages of 6 and 14 months. However, during my time teaching I discovered that those children who didn't sign so much as younger babies had what we termed a 'signing explosion' at around 14 months of age. All at once it seemed everything clicked into place and they had an awful lot to 'say'. The signs we had consistently been showing them were suddenly evident. So don't give up, you never know what is going to spark your child's interest.

For some, this will be almost as soon as you begin showing them the signs; for others, it may be further down the line. In the meantime, your baby will get a great deal of benefit from simply being signed to in the early stages. This is a sometimes underestimated stage of the process, which is actually very valuable for your baby. It is important not to be discouraged in any way, but to be consistent in the signs, knowing that you are encouraging communication and strengthening the bond between you and your baby.

> REMEMBER: Babies can take just a week or several months before making their first sign, so it is crucial to remember that many benefits of baby signing are achieved long before your baby may use her own signs.

You may hear some amazing and amusing stories of the moment a baby uses her first sign. Some children will be textbook examples of signing 'milk' or 'more' early. Others may begin earlier or later. A few babies (whose parents have been consistent with signing) have been known to sign very little, but have, however, begun to speak earlier than most, with their first words being those that have been signed to them. A baby's initial attempts at signing may not be what you have shown her. For example, quite often the 'more' sign may end up with a child patting the back of her hand – this being a rough approximation of what she has been shown, but adjusted due to her dexterity level. You will begin to notice how your child interprets different signs and uses them in context – but more on recognizing your baby's first sign just a little later...

For other babies, 'milk', 'more' or 'eat' isn't the first sign used. 'Duck' for some reason seems to be a favourite, but many babies will choose an animal sign as their first sign, such as Laila in the following example.

At 11 months Laila was on holiday with her family in Portugal. One of the Portuguese neighbours had a huge number of dogs tethered outside his house, which frequently erupted into a wild display of barking and howling, day and night. After a few days of hearing this, Laila's first sign to her mum was obviously 'dog'.

It is important to try not to put any pressure on your baby to sign early. Your aim should be to make the most of communication at this wonderful and charming stage of development and encourage your baby's sense of wonder and enjoyment.

We had been through a whole term of signing classes and Sasha was 11 months. She absolutely adored every lesson and was the noisiest of all the babies, especially when Jessie Cat made an appearance! She still wasn't signing though and we were wondering if she ever would. We went away on holiday and as I let the bath out and my husband put her in her pyjamas, I was taking my time and she

You will find many illustrations of other parents' experiences of
signing with their baby throughout this book. These are to inspire
and encourage you, and to highlight the fact that no two babies
are the same – everybody's signing story is different. You will find
a great diversity among parents' accounts and hopefully some will
ring true for you and your family.

Jane's second son began signing earlier than his brother (see the
box on page 21), but only used a few signs up until the age of
about 14 months. To begin with his mum wondered why, as she
thought she was far more natural with him with regard to her
speech and signing than she had been with her first son, and so
therefore far more effective.

One possible reason for her second son using so few signs early on
was that, being a second-time mum, Jane was much more aware
of his needs, and was very good at anticipating them. Therefore
he had little reason to express his needs to his mother, as she was
probably already well on the way to fulfilling them! Her first son
signed 'milk' for the first time purely because she had forgotten to
give it to him at his usual time.

So don't get disheartened if your child is taking a while to begin
signing, it may purely be that you are a superb parent readily
anticipating your child's every need. Be patient and consistent, and
your child will eventually have something to 'say' to you.

Insight

Remember, even if your baby is not signing, you can be sure
that in using some key word signs with your speech you are
giving your baby a head start in communication.

The advantages to your child begin the very first day you sign 'more?' This is because in the early stages of baby signing parents are inclined to:

- ▶ *speak more slowly so their baby can focus on what they are saying*
- ▶ *think about their child's understanding at a one-word level*
- ▶ *focus on their baby's thought processes and interests*
- ▶ *seek eye contact and shared looking*
- ▶ *repeat key words*
- ▶ *use a sign to draw their baby's attention to the key word of a sentence.*

This concentrated language input sparks connections of understanding and recognition in a baby's developing brain at a very early stage. Babies understand more of what is said to them and they enjoy extra parental attention. The joys of a baby's first sign are the parent's reward, but the babies themselves are reaping enormous developmental benefit from day one.

> REMEMBER: If you are using a few signs as part of your daily routine your baby will be listening, watching and learning gradually by your example, while taking great strides in understanding and vocabulary.

Many parents are great at communicating with their children – most will naturally chat to them about all sorts of things. As we are aware, this is good for their development and speech, but what some people aren't so aware of is that the constant dialogue, although very pleasing for children, isn't always the best way for them to learn to speak. It is also important to vary your speech between plenty of dialogue, so your child can understand the ebb and flow of language, and simplified sentences to get the message across.

Insight

Initially I was one of those parents who would chat away to their child, not realizing he really needed me to slow down and focus on just one main word within the sentence.

Once I learnt to speak directly at him, highlighting specific words as well as giving a visual sign, he learnt to sign and speak those highlighted words.

When simplifying a sentence you should sign one word within the sentence, recognizing that a child of that age is still understanding at a mono-word level. So, instead of saying 'Look, there, did you see that bird in the tree, just up there in the tree'. You would say 'Look, a *bird*,' (emphasizing the word but also signing *bird*), 'there is a *bird* up there in the tree'. You will find this naturally slows down your speech and enables your child to understand and begin to try to say and sign the word 'bird'.

Signing has been the most rewarding and useful class I have ever done. I have been able to understand my daughter's wants and needs from an early age (about 12 months) and her speech is just incredible! I have silenced all the critics and non-believers in friends and family and can't recommend it highly enough!

Philippa Mitchell, mum to Paige

Babies will be benefiting enormously from this signing input, but it is not as obvious and immediately rewarding for parents as the next stage, when their baby uses a sign themselves.

Recognizing your baby's first signs

The early signs your baby produces may only be rough approximations of the ones you have shown. This is because, as in all levels of their development, children develop at different rates, so their motor skills and dexterity levels may vary from other children of the same age. For example, a baby may use the sign for 'more' by tapping one hand on the back of the other, or even on the forearm. Some even just clap their hands together or attempt some other variation. This is to be expected is and completely normal. The accuracy of a baby's hand shapes when signing is not important at all; it is the message that counts.

HOW SHOULD I RESPOND IF I THINK MY BABY HAS STARTED SIGNING?

If you think you have seen a sign used in context then praise your baby by repeating the word in question while modelling the sign correctly. You can also use the opportunity to create meaning from your baby's gesture by allowing your baby to witness the cause and effect of her hand shapes, for example, 'When I clap, Daddy gives me more; if I want more, all I have to do is clap!' Don't be tempted to adapt your version of the sign to match your baby's. You should be consistent and your baby will refine the sign to match your own over time.

Our signing teacher told us that children vary in how long they take to sign – for Abigail it was one week! The teacher said she thought it was a record and naturally I glowed with maternal pride. She had in fact spent that first week making 'conducting' gestures every time she saw her radio but I didn't really take any notice – until the following week at class when she started 'conducting' every time the singing started. It was the teacher who pointed out that she was doing the sign for music! She'd picked up on the sign but I completely hadn't. I am amazed at just how much she understands and is aware of – so often we assume that because babies can't speak it means they can't understand speech, but how wrong we can be.

Jane Warden, mum to Abigail

USING THE SAME SIGN FOR DIFFERENT THINGS

When a child first starts signing, they may use a particular sign in context at some times and at other times use the same sign to communicate about something else. You may be thrilled when your baby points at the duck in the bath and uses the correct sign, but be somewhat confused when hours later she uses the same sign for your dog! It may seem that your baby is signing meaninglessly, but it is a very common phenomenon and follows exactly the same pattern as a baby's first spoken word. For example, many children will use one word (such as 'mama') for many things; so, too, will some children begin by using one sign to mean many different ideas. This is no bad thing. Your baby has just made a tremendous breakthrough in realizing that the gestures you are using do indeed stand for something and can be used to get something. Think about that again for a moment: your baby has just understood the concept that a word and sign mean something, and if she repeats that back to you, she may well get what she is wanting! Continue showing them other signs, remain consistent with the signs you are showing, and you will soon see that she begins to use the proper signs in the appropriate context.

REMEMBER: Language can be confusing to a baby!

Another reason why your baby may be using the same sign for lots of different objects or concepts is because our wonderful language can be confusing. How often do we say 'Do you want *that* toy?', 'Can you see *that* train?', 'Do you want *that* drink?' or '*That's* a sheep'? Do you see the pattern? Often, without realizing it, we are reinforcing the word *that* – our children then interpret the sign and use it for a huge variety of objects.

Top tip

An easy way to avoid confusion in the early stages of signing is to repeat back the word you are signing: 'Do you want that *car*, the *car*?' This not only helps reinforce the sign you are using, but enables your baby to listen again to the word associated with the sign.

It seems that after mastering a few signs, most babies suddenly realize that signing will get them what they desire or are curious about, and their ability to retain signs becomes evident. The other aspect you will then begin to notice is your baby refining her attempts to get her message across. As this all falls into place many parents see an 'explosion' of their baby's signing.

We starting signing when Lilli-Rose was four months. She used to sit and watch me, and I became a little disheartened that she didn't sign. I only kept up a few signs – 'more', 'all finished', 'please' and 'thank you'. Just after a year she suddenly started doing all of them, in relation to almost everything she wanted to tell me, for example 'more' playing, reading, food, drink, etc. I wished I had kept up more signs!

Julia

Case study

Catherine's second son was a very early signer. By the time he came along, the family had got into the habit of signing with his older brother, so they thought they were almost naturally signing from birth. As he signed early, they were expecting him to continue very quickly picking up the signs, just as his brother had done – after all, they were showing him so many signs. However, over the next eight to nine months he maintained around ten basic signs, which the family found a little disconcerting. Nevertheless they continued, because they knew from experience of being in baby-signing classes that at around a year old, many babies, whatever age they start signing, will really take off and have a 'signing explosion'.

Their son reached a year, and still he continued with the same basic signs. Then around 14 and a half months he really had a 'signing explosion' and all of a sudden he was rapidly using many of the signs which he had been taught over the months! He had obviously been taking in everything that was being shown to him, and now it seemed all of a sudden he had a lot to 'tell' everyone, and wanted to ensure that he was understood. Sometimes he would give his parents a questioning look, as he watched or noticed something new, and his parents began to become aware of what new things he wanted the word and the accompanying sign for. One of the additional benefits the family observed with the boys was that they could recognize things and were able to effectively communicate (sign) different concepts to people, now they just needed to try out the word. Soon after this, their son began to drop some of the early signs in favour of speaking those very same words that had been signed to him. Catherine and the rest of the family began to understand the importance of clearly saying the word that was being signed, and as a result noticed it really helped with both their boys' speech development.

We will expand a little more on the effectiveness of naming objects, and the head start you are giving your baby in Chapter 7: 'Signing with older children'.

Getting started – your first basic signs

By now you may well have read about what baby signing is, how it started, when you should start signing, when your baby will begin to sign back to you, and how you will recognize her first sign – or you may have jumped to this section and want to know the actual nuts and bolts of signing with your baby. With all parents we recommend using the ten basic guidelines:

BASIC GUIDELINE NO. 1: BEGIN WITH BASICS SUCH AS 'EAT', 'DRINK', 'MILK', 'MORE' AND 'ALL GONE' (FINISHED)

We would recommend using these signs first, as they are signs that you can use many times during the day – they are an undemanding way to initiate signing. Start by trying to use the signs just at mealtimes, as this will be a routine already familiar with you and an easy place to start (and you can be sure you are following guideline no. 7 by being consistent!).

EAT

Bear in mind you can view all of these signs on the CD-ROM accompanying the book. However, for ease, I am going to explain the first sign.

How to sign it
Bunch your fingertips together and gently tap the corner of your mouth as you emphasize saying the word 'eat'.

When to use it
When you have just finished preparing your baby's meal, you could say 'Would you like to *eat*?' as you use the sign. Pop your baby into her chair, finish attaching her bib, and say again 'Would you like to *eat*?' Repeat the sign every time you say the word. As you put down her bowl, or offer her the spoon you can sign and say 'Time to *eat* now'. Alternatively, you can use the word you are most comfortable with: food, lunchtime, snack, etc. However, at this point and age of development, the generic word 'eat' is sufficient for your baby.

Figure 2.1 Eat.

Insight

Be relaxed about starting to sign with your child. If your child is obviously hungry and desperate for food, don't stop at that point to sign! Give a few mouthfuls and then show her the sign for 'eat' or maybe 'more'.

REMEMBER: Always say the word as you sign it. Never sign in silence.

MORE

How to sign it
Make a fist with one hand, and then with the other hand flat, cover it over the top of the fist, as if you were pushing a cork into a bottle. Say 'more'.

Figure 2.2 More.

When to use it
When you have given your baby a few mouthfuls of food, you could stop and say 'Would you like some *more*?' You could continue with this, as a game with your baby. Offer a few more mouthfuls, then keep stopping and ask if she would like some '*more*'.

Sam began signing when he was nine months old. He soon
started asking for 'more' and trying other signs.

Sam's cousin, Maddy, started signing classes after we had been
singing its praises. His grandma took him to visit Maddy and a
lot of effort was put into trying to get Sam to sign something.
He decided he was not going to show off his skills.

They fed the ducks, he just ate the bread.

They waved at people, he just smiled.

Everyone gave up and had afternoon tea. As soon as he was
given some cheesecake to eat he started to sign 'more' and
would not stop! Even when it was all gone he kept asking for
'more' cheesecake!

His aunt and uncle had not seen a baby sign and thought it was
great. It made them more determined to carry on with the lessons.

Su Boardman

DRINK

'Drink' and 'milk' are very easy first signs as well as being signs that can be used many times in a day.

How to sign it
Shape your hand as if you were holding a beaker, lift it a few times to your mouth, and say the word 'drink'.

Figure 2.3 Drink.

When to use it
If you are signing with a young baby of around six to 16 months, we would recommend using the 'drink' sign whether it be for water, juice, or whatever drink you choose to give your baby. Some people like to ask their baby if they are thirsty and then use the drink sign. But it is only when they are slightly older that it can be useful to start giving them choices. We will cover giving your baby choices a little more in Chapter 7, but at this point it is important to consider we are aiming for simplicity, as this is the key to beginning successful signing with your baby.

MILK

The same sign can be used for 'milk' whether you are breast- or
bottle-feeding.

How to sign it
*Make a fist, then open and close your fist as if you are milking a
cow. Say the word 'milk'.*

Figure 2.4 Milk.

For those mums who are dual feeding, i.e. using breast and bottle milk, and want a way to differentiate between bottle and breast feeding, an alternative suggestion for milk is for mum to tap both hands just above their chest for 'mummy milk'.

My first daughter Neve joined a signing class in London when she was six months old in 2004. It was a brand new class, and baby signing felt very cutting edge at the time. Needless to say, my friends and family were impressed by the concept, but I could tell they were waiting for 'results' before getting enthusiastic. They did not have to wait long.

After only one term, Neve visited her grandparents in Portugal for a spot of sunshine. She became very poorly with the local tummy-bug and I was at my wits' end. She was lying listlessly on her grandma's lap, exhausted and dehydrated, and as I came into the room, she looked at me with desperation in her eyes and did a strong clear 'milk' sign! We were thrilled! We gave her a drink, and she soon perked up.

Vanessa Kreimeia, mother to Neve and Laila

It is probably important to reiterate that although these are the first basic signs to start using with your child, they may not be the first signs she shows you. Babies will start signing what they are interested in, or something they want to tell you. These signs are great to get you used to signing many times a day with your baby, but don't only show your baby these signs and wait for her to sign back to you before progressing with more signs. If you are in a good routine with your baby, and she is used to food, milk and naps at specific times, then you might find you are so perfectly meeting her needs that she has no need to ask you for milk or a drink at this stage. So, don't give up if your baby isn't signing back these basic signs to you. Keep showing her more signs, watching what she is interested in – maybe it's animals, or anything with wheels.

Laura found her son's first sign was 'light'. This would be a more unusual sign for a baby to begin with, but beautifully illustrates the point of showing your baby many different signs and focusing on what they are interested in. Laura had been signing all the first basic signs, such as 'eat' and 'drink', for several weeks but with no response from her son Luke. Then she noticed that he always looked up at lights in a room – so, watching his cues, she started signing it to him. Within a few days Luke had cottoned on. Laura said it was fantastic to be able to communicate and understand in what his little mind was interested.

During the course of this book you will find many different signs to show your baby, and plenty more on the accompanying CD-ROM. Watch what she is interested in, or pointing at, and aim to give her the appropriate sign.

ALL GONE/FINISHED

How to sign it
Begin by holding your fists together with your palms facing inwards, then move your hands out so your hands are flat and facing down. Say 'all gone'.

Figure 2.5 All gone.

When to use it

'All gone' or 'finished' is a versatile sign to use many times throughout the day, not only at mealtimes. When you have finished feeding, your peek-a-boo game is over, the story book you were reading to your baby has finished, when a TV programme has ended, or a visitor leaves the house, try using the 'all gone' (finished) sign.

When you have to disappoint your baby because something is over, this sign is unequivocal. Using the 'all gone' sign consistently will help your baby overcome the many little disappointments she faces. You may not believe it until you try it, but it works! 'All gone' is often one of the first signs to be initiated by babies.

Insight

The more you use a certain sign, the more likely it is that your baby will start to recognize it in context and anticipate what is about to happen. Get in the habit of using these signs and aim to adopt them as a natural and habitual part of daily routines. Repetition and consistency is the key to successful baby signing.

BASIC GUIDELINE NO. 2: FOLLOW YOUR BABY'S LEAD

Watch carefully to see what interests your baby and follow her lead. From nine months onwards, particularly, begin to introduce signs for those words your baby might want to say, or is beginning to point at.

Each baby has different interests and while one enthusiastically points to and gets excited by anything to do with wheels, another may be fascinated by the family cat or the swings in the park. You know your child, and you know what other signs will be the most motivating for her. As your baby points to something of interest, then looks back to you, start showing her the relevant signs. Babies and children generally have an insatiable appetite for learning more about the world around them and will therefore require more signs to satisfy their ever-increasing needs, desires and curiosities.

BASIC GUIDELINE NO. 3: ALWAYS SAY THE WORD AS YOU SIGN

This is especially significant, and an area where Sing and Sign differs from some American and English programmes, which advocate maintaining some form of silent communication. Clearly, your child will not want to hear your lovely voice from morning until night, and there will be times when you may sit quietly having a cuddle, or just gathering your thoughts (if that is at all possible with a young baby). However, when you are communicating with your baby, and using a sign, you must always say the word.

Insight
Our aim when using a sign is to encourage and develop our children's speech, which cannot be achieved when using the sign alone. Therefore it cannot be overstated how important it is *always* to say the word as you sign it.

By doing this, you are giving your child verbal and visual encouragement to communicate with you. Your child will pick up the visual clue, but also clearly hear the word behind the sign. This is why the words that you sign are often your baby's first spoken words.

BASIC GUIDELINE NO. 4: SPEAK SLOWLY, BUT NATURALLY

Try to speak a little slower than usual but in a natural way, maintaining eye contact if possible. As you adjust your speech slightly, you will give your child a greater chance to pick up on and process exactly what you are saying. Many parents can be great at providing their child with rich language in large quantities, speaking at a regular speed. This is a vital part of exposing your child to variety in language. However, when you begin to sign with your child, it is recommended that you sign just the one word in a sentence. You will find this will slow your speech down, and enable your child to begin speaking the words you are signing. Often, children whose parents have practised baby signing will do this earlier than their (non-signing) peers.

> **REMEMBER: Don't slow your speech down to the point where it becomes stilted, but certainly slow it down enough to speak the specific word you are signing and to repeat it if necessary.**

Eye contact and facial expressions provide important social and emotional information. People, perhaps without consciously doing so, probe each other's eyes and faces for positive or negative mood signs. Eye contact shows personal involvement and creates intimate bonds. Recent studies also suggest that eye contact has a positive impact on the retention and recall of information and may promote more efficient learning.

Some parents will not realize the full benefit of maintaining good eye contact with a young baby. One parent remarked that it wasn't until she had an active toddler on her hands, who wanted to be, and do, everything, that she suddenly began realizing the wisdom of what she had been teaching her baby. When the baby became a much stronger-willed toddler, his earlier training meant it was much more natural for the parent to have hold of him, on his level, maintaining good eye contact with him, while giving him instruction, or indeed just telling him how much she loved him! The message that you are imparting always penetrates that much deeper when maintaining good eye contact.

BASIC GUIDELINE NO. 5: KEEP IT SIMPLE

Use just one sign per sentence when speaking with your baby. The more signs you learn, the more tempted you may be to use more than you need. But the magic of baby signing lies in its simplicity. You can use as many interesting signs as you like with your baby – but *only one per sentence*. For example, you may see a cat in your garden and want to draw your baby's attention to it. You would continue to speak normally, saying and signing 'Look, do you see that little *cat*. Look, it's just about to climb the big fir tree. Can you see the little *cat*?' The main focus for your baby's attention is the cat, so although you may know the signs for 'little', 'big' and 'tree' and have effectively used them on many other occasions, it is important to keep in mind the key word approach with your baby at this stage of development.

> **REMEMBER: Just use one sign per sentence.** Your child may get
> to the point where she begins signing more than one word per
> sentence, showing off her skills, but you should maintain your
> stance of using one sign per sentence.

The exception to this rule is when signing along to action songs, as
you will often use more than one sign in each phrase of the song
and will therefore have the opportunity to practise your fluency
and co-ordination. So while you learn signs from songs, your baby
will learn gradually and naturally from your everyday exchanges,
and the signs you use in context at home.

BASIC GUIDELINE NO. 6: HAPPILY ACCEPT ANY SIGNING ATTEMPTS BY YOUR BABY

Even approximate imitations of the signs you show should be
accepted. As we have already discussed in 'Recognizing your baby's
first signs' on page 27, you may not get an exact representation of
the sign you are showing your baby. A perfect sign is not what we
are trying to achieve. Increased communication between you and
your baby is a far better ideal to aim for. As long as you recognize
the sign your baby is giving you, and the meaning your baby attaches
to that sign, then show your baby lots of enthusiasm and praise for
attempting to sign. This usually comes naturally to most parents who
cannot contain their excitement at their baby's first sign!

BASIC GUIDELINE NO. 7: BE CONSISTENT

Be consistent in how you show a sign, however your baby
adapts it. If you are consistent in using the signs you have chosen,
your baby will be noticing, listening and learning gradually by
your example while taking great strides in comprehension and
vocabulary. You may think that if your baby uses the 'more' sign,
for instance, by tapping her forearm (instead of the hand coming
down to cover the fist) that you should copy her interpretation
of the sign. However, this will greatly confuse your baby who is
used to seeing you use the sign correctly. In general, the more your
baby sees you sign, or sees a particular sign, the quicker she will

recognize it, and the quicker she will learn it and therefore start using it for herself.

BASIC GUIDELINE NO. 8: AVOID TRYING TO GET YOUR BABY TO 'PERFORM' SIGNS

As excited as you may be when your child has begun signing, avoid the temptation of making her perform. Signing should remain fun for you and your child, and an easy way to communicate. It should not have the added pressure of pleasing an audience, however appreciative that audience may be. The more natural you are when signing with your child and the more your child has to say, the more she will naturally sign. Family and friends are bound to notice your baby signing once she starts.

BASIC GUIDELINE NO. 9: BE PATIENT AND RELAXED ABOUT BABY SIGNING

Enjoy the process of communicating with your child, regardless of her signing attempts. Signing can become a natural part of your communication with your child so try and maintain a relaxed approach. Think about the most popular sign or gesture parents often use with their child – waving hello or goodbye. This is often done enthusiastically, signing and saying the word, without any embarrassment of what others might think of them. This is how all signing should be with your child – easy, effortless and natural. Again, begin with the basics and gradually build up your signs, signing whenever possible.

Remember, signing with your baby should be fun, giving you time to focus on things your baby may enjoy or be interested in.

BASIC GUIDELINE NO. 10: PRAISE, PRAISE, PRAISE!

We all know how well people, and especially children, respond to praise and encouragement. If you think you have seen a sign used in context then praise your baby, however fragile the attempt.

You can also take this opportunity to repeat the word and the sign back to your baby, ensuring, of course, that you are consistent with your sign, and modelling it correctly. If your baby's attempts at signing are rewarded with the response she wanted, she will be far more motivated to learn more signs, therefore enhancing your communication with your baby even further.

Insight

These first basic signs are great to begin using in your daily routines as you feed, change and bathe and put your baby to bed. See how many times you can incorporate them into your day to build up your ease and confidence with signing. As you move forward in the book you will learn some more fun motivational signs for your baby.

TEST YOUR KNOWLEDGE

1 *What is a good age to begin baby signing?*

2 *Why is this a good age to begin signing?*

3 *Name three (out of a possible ten) guidelines for successful signing.*

4 *When parents begin signing with their baby they are often giving them a head start in communicating. Give one reason why this might be the case.*

5 *How many signs should you include when you are talking to your baby?*

6 *What is the exception to the above rule?*

7 *At what age will your baby begin to sign to you?*

8 *Give one reason why a baby who is beginning to sign may use the same sign for many things.*

9 *Why is it important always to say the word as you sign it?*

10 *If your baby gives her own interpretation of a sign, how should you respond?*

See answer section at the back of the book.

3

The next steps

In this chapter you will learn:
- *how to use signs within your established routines*
- *signs which may be motivating for your child*
- *simple songs to use when preparing to go out or change your child's nappy*
- *ideas for implementing signs at home.*

Introducing signs relevant to your child's world

At this point, you are hopefully mastering the first basic signs of 'eat', 'drink', 'milk', 'more' and 'all gone' – and beginning to use those signs many times during the day. Keep in mind that mealtimes are a great time to use all of the first basic signs. Maybe your baby has begun to recognize them and respond when you use them, or maybe your baby is already starting to use them. Whatever stage you are at, keep persevering with signing – remember, you may not be able to see the benefits at this stage, but you will be expanding your baby's language and comprehension.

Insight
Some parents have found it helpful when first learning the basic signs to print them out and have them easily accessible.

The next five signs will also fit the same category and be signs that will be used frequently during the day. There is no harm in using as many signs as you can remember. Using these signs as descriptive gestures to support some of these important words will help your baby understand and remember what they mean.

Early basics: 'where', 'help', 'open', 'no', 'yes'

WHERE

When to use it
A fun way to introduce other family members to your baby's signing is through playing simple hiding games with cuddly toys. Grandparents especially love to play and interact with their grandchildren. Begin by showing them a simple game using the 'where' sign.

Most babies love to play 'peek-a-boo' and in fact any game that involves finding a favourite toy. 'Where' is one of those gestures that many parents will naturally use with their baby.

Insight

'Where' is one of the most common first signs among babies in class. They love Jessie Cat who hides away in a colourful box – they can then 'ask' the question 'Where, oh where, oh where is Jessie?' The delight and anticipation on their faces is wonderful. It is a game they never seem to tire of, and something simple to play at home with your baby, too.

How to sign it
Hold your hands in front of you with palms facing upwards, making small circles. Say 'where'.

Figure 3.1 Where.

> The most fun sign with Jacob is 'where'. He loves to hide things (or himself) and sign 'where' before popping back out with a 'boo'!
>
> Chris with Jacob, aged one

If your baby is enjoying playing a hiding game with you then use the 'where' sign when the cuddly toy has been hidden, and of course the 'more' sign if your baby is enjoying the game. When it's time to stop, you can also make use of the 'all gone' or 'finished' sign.

> Ben adopted the 'where' sign very quickly after he starting signing (aged 13 months) and has used it, enthusiastically, to play hide-and-seek-games with his parents and other relatives ever since. He has been able to take the lead in hiding an object and telling his family to do the seeking (using the 'where' sign), enabling him to communicate proactively, developing his confidence and displaying a cheeky sense of humour in a way that, without signing, would have been impossible at such a young age.
>
> Jane Kirkby and Ben

HELP

Many babies like the 'help' sign and it is a useful sign that can significantly reduce frustration, especially with a child desperate to achieve something, but who is unable to do so without some added input.

How to sign it
With outstretched arms, make the thumbs up sign with your right hand, put this hand on top of your upturned left palm, then move both hands together towards your chest. Say 'help'.

Figure 3.2 Help.

When to use it
As your child becomes more independent there will be more things during a day he may need your help with. Maybe he is trying to reach for an object or stack some blocks and they keep falling.

He may be older and trying to put his shoes on. You can say 'Shall I *help* you with...?', clearly demonstrating the 'help' sign. It won't be long before your baby or toddler will be using the sign to ask for your help.

Case study

CASE STUDY

Michelle was interacting with her young daughter when Melissa began frantically signing 'help' to her mum. Michelle, quickly recognizing her daughter's sign and increasing frustration, went over to her and said and signed:

'What? Melissa, what do you want help with?'

Melissa then quickly signed 'rabbit' followed by 'where'. Her mum again quickly responded with 'Oh, you want to know where your rabbit is? I tidied up and put it in the toy box.' With that, it was taken out of the toy box and returned to a very happy Melissa, who then sat cuddling her favourite rabbit.

Note how this short interaction between Melissa and her mum enabled Melissa simply yet effectively to communicate her needs to her mother, and how straightforward it was for her mother to decipher her daughter's desires. Many non-signing babies have similar wants – finding a favourite cuddly toy, or other prized possession – but the outcome could have been very different. If Mum didn't understand baby's pointing, grunting and possibly crying, it could result in escalating frustration and, for some no doubt, a full-blown temper tantrum. This is a true-life example of how signing can help and aid simple communication with your baby.

Insight

I love this interaction between Michelle and Melissa. I think it is one of those classic examples of the beauty of baby signing and how using such simple gestures can make such a huge difference in the family.

OPEN

'Open' is another particularly useful sign to use with your baby, and so easy too.

How to sign it
Just scrunch your hand up, and with a big flourish, open your fingers out. Say 'open'.

When to use it
This sign is particularly good for facial expressiveness and should be said with a nice, high, light voice. As well as being easy for babies' hands to master, 'open' is a sign that really motivates because the resulting reward is instant, especially if you are about to give your baby a treat. Whenever you open something that your baby is about to enjoy, such as a yoghurt or a toy box, use the sign to show him what you are doing.

Insight

If you want to play a great game with your baby, incorporating the 'open', 'where', and 'all gone' signs, why not use a pillowcase or bag to hide a few favourite toys? Ask your baby 'Where is...?' Surprisingly quickly, babies enter into the game and point to the pillowcase or bag. This is the ideal time to use the 'open' sign, and produce the toy with a great flourish. Repeat the game while your baby maintains interest, using the 'more' sign. Don't forget to use the 'all gone' sign at the end of the game.

NO

This 'no' sign is wonderful as it illustrates perfectly the expressiveness of a simple gesture, and a very clear message is present in the body language.

How to sign it
Use a flat hand facing away from your body, and make one movement starting in front of your body, taking your hand out to the side. Say 'no' clearly.

Figure 3.3 No.

When to use it
Use this sign any time you are using such language as 'no', 'don't touch', 'mustn't', etc.

You can also leave the sign in the air, while the message of what you are saying sinks in. By recommending you use a clear and consistent 'no' sign, we are not in any way encouraging you to be negative with your baby. Generally, it is always better to put something in a positive rather than a negative way with your child. However, there are times when a 'don't touch' is appropriate, for instance, if a child is about to touch something hot.

Insight
With my sons I tried hard not to use the word 'no' as I had heard many parents complain this was their child's first word. They would see the 'no' sign and hear 'don't touch' on a regular basis. Another good tip is, after using this sign, to instruct your child to 'come away' while beckoning to them. This is helpful in removing your child from the temptation and giving you the ability to engage them in another activity.

As Chloe has become more mobile, I have had to use the sign and say the word 'no' more often. Chloe clearly understands the sign and tone of voice I use. Often, all I have to do is say her name and say 'no', and she will look at me and repeat the sign before moving on to something else.

Jeanette Luck

Some people find that their baby is very adaptable to signing – for example, while many babies' first word might be 'no', the signing child might quickly learn this sign as an alternative form of protest.

Top tip

If your baby likes to head towards the fireplace or other dangerous items in your house that are impossible to move and that are therefore out of bounds, try calling his name when he heads towards it and clearly saying 'Don't touch', adding the 'no' sign. Try leaving your hand in the air for a few moments in order for the visual cue to continue after you have said the words – this will leave your baby in no doubt about what you are saying.

Finn was 11 months old and walking confidently. Typically, he was into absolutely everything including a freestanding bedside lamp. The 'no' sign is obviously a well-used sign and my baby in his attempt to grab the lamp and pull it over, was told 'no' using the sign. To my amazement he signed it back to me, with a great big grin on his face. Not only was he now signing, he was using it with humour! Finn's signing has now taken off and all members of the family use it readily and with confidence.

Julie Neville with Finn

The 'no' gesture covers a wide range of words and can help your baby's growing understanding of everyday language such as 'don't', 'mustn't', 'didn't', 'none', 'never', 'nothing', 'no more'... This list could go on and on, but the sign is the same and is very simple. This is another example of using a generic sign to cover many words, and the essential principal of keeping signing simple with your baby.

> **REMEMBER: Even when your baby is older and able to talk and say the word 'no', this remains one of those very useful signs that is worth continuing to sign with your child.**

Parents have often commentated on how useful they found using the 'no' sign, especially at busy parent and child type activities when their lively toddler was across the other side of a room. Without seeming to be parents who shout at their children, they could shout their child's name to gain their attention, and then sign 'no' while trying to reach them. It would often stop them in their tracks long enough to avoid a difficult or dangerous situation. Eventually, you may be able to use the sign without needing to move from your chair. If you get into the habit of using the 'no' sign you will find the sign does the shouting for you.

Case study

Maya is 11 months old and we have been going to baby signing for a number of weeks.

I was looking forward to teaching her the signs but the only one she has got is 'no'. And I know the exact moment she learnt it. I was trying to stop her climbing on the cabinet to the TV and she had previously responded to a verbal 'no' after I had taken her away several times. After a while, she pushed the boundaries and grinned at me as she edged to the telly.

I let her go so far and then said 'no' and signed it clearly, looking her in the eye. She started to cry a little and I told her why she couldn't. And again put my hand up. Instead of crying she sat and stared at me for a clear minute. I ignored her. For about a month after she was grouchy with me and became a daddy's girl and I worried that I had gone too far and maybe broken our bond.

Today we were playing really happily and she had had enough of dinner, she had been closing her mouth but I wasn't sure if she was just messing or hadn't finished the last mouthful. She obviously got fed up. Looking totally exasperated, she signed 'no' and shook her head. I laughed and told her it was OK if she had finished.

She looked so happy to be finally understood, and to have a voice of her own that mummy also respected. I think our bond is stronger than ever.

Tara Mills

Insight

One of my sons was (and still is) very strong willed. He would go to the fireplace, then when he had my attention, he would sign 'no' (or 'don't touch' as we used to say) and then put his hands directly on the cold coals. Because he was signing to us in this way, it showed us he knew and understood the instruction. Now we needed to quickly assess how we were going to handle such an active choice of disobedience, something we hadn't considered when he was only ten months of age.

YES

'Yes' is possibly not a sign that your young baby will use early on, but goes hand-in-hand with the 'no' sign, so this is therefore a useful place in the book to show you this sign.

How to sign it
Make a fist with your right hand and 'nod' yes (from your wrist) with your hand. Say 'yes', at the same time.

Figure 3.4 Yes.

When to use it

'Yes' is a sign that is often used when giving your baby choices: 'Would you like a breadstick – yes?' You will find you can use it many times with lift-the-flap books: 'Who is under rug? Is it the dog? Yes – there he is!' Older babies and toddlers love to use this sign when asked a question. The earlier you expose your baby to this sign and establish its meaning, the earlier he will understand and begin to take advantage of using the sign. For some babies this will be interlinked with their verbal communication.

With younger babies, begin by emphasizing the word 'yes' at a time when you are confident this is their likely answer to a question, for example 'Would you like an apple/chocolate biscuit?' If their eyes light up at the thought of food, introduce the sign within your sentence: 'Yes – you would like an apple.'

It shouldn't be too long before your baby is trying the sign or to say the word. Bear in mind, however, that this is very age dependant – a younger child's 'yes' may simply come out as a 'sssssss'. Once your child has grasped the concept of what 'yes' means, you might like to try moving on to what we would call at this age a 'parent-pleasing sign' – 'please'.

If your child has appropriately responded to the question 'Would you like an apple?' by either signing, or saying 'yes', this is a fitting time to introduce the word and sign 'please' (you can see this sign in Chapter 4, 'Love and manners'). This continues to keep your signing at a one-word focus level, which is age appropriate, but moves your baby on to introduce further concepts and ideas. When you do this your baby may start to sign just the word 'please' if he wants something. However, it is important to note, at this point of development, manners are far more important to parents than babies, which is why signs such as 'please' and 'thank you' are referred to as parent-pleasers. This is in no way negating the importance of manners, but recognizes that the relevance for a six-month-old won't be the same as for an 18-month-old with a wider vocabulary and understanding. Babies will sign what they are interested in, so signs that incorporate manners tend to come

much further down the list and are generally used mainly with
older babies.

Routines: going out, nappy changing, bath and bed

We all know how much babies love and thrive on routines.
In this next section, we will be using straightforward concepts
and simple themes that will begin to extend your baby's growing
understanding. All the concepts and themes are based on the
vocabulary of your baby's world. By using additional signs
during everyday events, you will be increasing your signing
repertoire, as well as providing your baby with concrete
illustrations of events that are about to happen. This in turn will
aid your baby's comprehension and eventually his vocabulary.

LET'S GO OUT

A baby's world is really quite small, so going out is a major
event and something babies will usually get excited about. Too
often we can make a decision to go to the shops, visit a friend,
walk the dog, and start packing the nappy bag, getting our shoes,
coat and even our baby's shoes on without our baby knowing
what is going on. We have failed to communicate with what we
are doing, and where we are going. Below are some of the basic
signs that are perfect at this age to incorporate into your going
out routine, ensuring your baby is calm and confident in knowing
what is coming next.

GOING OUT

How to sign it
Cup your hand slightly, palm facing downwards, and mime 'going over the wall' – remembering to say 'we are going out'.

Figure 3.5 Going out.

When to use it
Use 'going out' to signal the beginning of preparations for departure. We recommend showing signs for the places you visit regularly – maybe it's the park, shops or swimming pool.

It might be worth noting at this point that all of these signs can be seen on the accompanying CD-ROM. However, some signs are so simple that they do not need pictures, so I will just provide a brief explanation.

SHOPS

How to sign it
With two hands starting close to your chest, mime pushing a trolley, so as you extend, 'push' your arms in front.

SWIMMING POOL

How to sign it
Mime doing breaststroke.

FARM

How to sign it
Think of a farmer wearing braces. With both thumbs, mime pulling braces forward.

MUSIC (CLASS)

How to sign it
With index fingers in the air, wave from side to side as if conducting.

PARK

How to sign it
With a flat hand facing downwards, make a wide circle from your waist.

When at the park, what does your baby enjoy doing? Maybe he loves being pushed on the swings, going fast down the slide, or perhaps there is a sandpit he loves to play in? As these are activities babies generally enjoy, they are highly motivating signs and therefore ones that many babies will use. Try to use these when at the park, or even in your own back garden.

SWINGS

How to sign it
Use both hands to mime a swing action by your sides. Remember to say 'swings'.

Figure 3.6 Swings.

SLIDE

How to sign it
Use a flat hand to mime sliding down.

SAND

How to sign it
Think of rubbing flour through your fingers. Do this action while raising your hands upwards, and saying 'sand'.

Figure 3.7 Sand.

We're going to the park
We're going to the park,
Ee-i-a-dio we're going to the park

> It's been fantastic to be able to know what our baby is thinking when we are walking down the street. He'll often stop to 'tell' us about some birds or flowers he has seen. Signing has brought a great richness to our relationship with Jacob and we feel very privileged to know him so well.
>
> Chris Miles with Jacob aged 12 months

As much as babies love to go out, sometimes it can be difficult getting them there. Communicating where you are going and what you are doing may generally make things easier, but sometimes not even that will help. The first thing you may begin a battle with is putting on their shoes or maybe their coat...

COAT

How to sign it
Mime pulling a coat around your shoulders. Remember to say 'coat'.

SHOES

How to sign it
With one hand make a 'bridge' and mime putting a 'shoe' on the other hand. Remember to say 'shoes'.

Figure 3.8 Shoes.

When to use it

Don't forget to use this sign as you are putting your baby's shoes on. You can then let him know if you are going for a walk – so you can use the sign for 'buggy' or 'going out' – or maybe this is a journey you are making on public transport or in the car. All are simple signs that you can incorporate into your signing repertoire.

BUGGY

How to sign it
Mime pushing a buggy in front of you.

BUS

How to sign it
With arms parallel to your shoulders and straight arms, mime a big steering wheel.

CAR

How to sign it
With hands in front of you and bent arms, mime a small steering wheel.

Wherever you are going, whatever you are doing, and however you are getting there, try to let your baby know as much as possible, using a few of these easy signs.

On getting ready to go out, you may find your conversation goes something like this:

'Come on then, we are *going out*.' Your child may look up at you, so you can respond to their look by replying, 'Yes, we are *going out*.' Pick up your child, or take him to where you can then begin to put his shoes on. Sitting him back down again, you can say 'Come on, let's put your *shoes* on.' This would be a great time to try out the song on page 63 to help you make this sometimes difficult time into a fun way of preparing to go out the door. Finally, with shoes, coat, bag and child all set, you can let them know you are going in the *buggy*, *bus* or the *car*. Once safely strapped in the buggy or the car (but before you drive off), it would be a good time to tell your child where you are going – the *park*, *shops*, the *swimming pool*, or maybe a *music class*. Use an appropriate sign and it won't be long before your child has an understanding of all the places you regularly visit and an ability to predict what comes next.

You may be surprised one day when you tell your toddler you are going out, that he simply signs *shoes* to you, or toddles off to get his own shoes. Many parents have testified to this type of scenario and have come to fully understand the value and power of using signs in context during everyday situations.

Insight

Children love order and routine, and even with such a simple thing as getting ready to go out, at an early age they can begin to predict what happens next and what is expected of them.

The value in signing to get over these sometimes difficult moments cannot be overstated. It somehow seems that doing things rhythmically gets children moving in a way that persuasion and even bribery cannot. You may be aware of the traditional nursery rhyme 'Here we go round the mulberry bush'. This can be sung as 'Here we go and put on our shoes' or 'Here we go…' doing practically anything! This song is great for fitting most things. It can be really beneficial when preparing to go out, making it so much easier and a lot more fun. Why not try it yourself?

> *This is the way we put on our* shoes
> *Put on our* shoes
> *Put on our* shoes.
> *This is the way we put on our* shoes
> *On a cold and frosty morning.*
> *This is the way we put on our* hat
> *Put on our* hat
> *Put on our* hat.
> *This is the way we put on our* hat
> *On a warm and sunny day-ay.*

HAT

How to sign it
With a flat hand, put a 'hat' on your head, by patting your head.

When to use it
This sign is great to use when you are going out on a hot summer's day or indeed when you are wrapping up warm and snug in winter months.

Your child may love going out, or walking down the road to the shops. However, for some it can become a huge trial. You may be a parent who has difficulty getting down the road because your toddler has other ideas. Playing simple games and using simple melodies such as 'walk and stop', 'march and stop', etc. can help you to complete an otherwise simple journey without too much difficulty. You can be inventive and make up your own words and tunes. Your baby will absolutely love your singing attempts, even if others would cover their ears!

HOME

'Home' is a particularly important sign: it represents a refuge and safe haven for your baby. Wherever you are, inevitably it will eventually be time to go 'home'.

How to sign it
Mime a roof, saying 'home' as your fingertips touch.

Figure 3.9 Home.

This is a simple sign, but eloquently provides your baby with a clear illustration of what is about to happen. Just as your going out routine provides your baby with the stability of being able to predict what comes next, don't forget to let him know when it is time to go home. For some babies, this sign is a welcome relief, and for others it can cause upset if they have to leave a favourite activity they have been enjoying. For Jess in the following example, it was a sign she used, but which wasn't understood.

My daughter was collected from nursery by her Nana and Grandad a few weeks ago. When they arrived she was sat with one of the workers while she waited, repeatedly doing a sign. They said they wished they knew what she had been trying to say, and showed me the sign... she had been signing 'home'.

Jo Mitchell and Jess

The above example not only illustrates how much babies can understand and how they can communicate their wishes, it also shows the importance of letting significant people in your baby's world know the signs he is using, so they can more appropriately respond to his needs. We will cover important people in your baby's world, and signing within a nursery setting, in a little more detail in Chapter 5.

We're going to the park
We're going to the park
Ee-i-a-dio we're going to the park,
And now we're going home
Now we're going home
Ee-i-a-dio, now we're going home.

NAPPY TIME

Another occurrence that takes place with alarming regularity in your baby's world is the endless changing of nappies. Before you pick your baby up to go and change his nappy, use this simple sign to let him know what you are going to do.

CHANGE (NAPPY)

How to sign it
*Hold your fists together and twist from side to side, saying 'change
your nappy'.*

Figure 3.10 Change nappy.

Some babies lie perfectly still – many wriggle and squirm.
Obviously, trying to sign and change a nappy at the same time is
not going to work, so in this instance you could try the trusted
routine of singing to your baby while changing: nappy time,
bathtime, why not use it as 'sing along time'? Even if you think
your singing is not up to scratch, your baby will love to hear it. It
is amazing that a simple solution, such as singing, can ease problem
areas when relating to your child.

This wonderfully simple nappy song can be sung to the tune of 'Frère Jacques'.

> **Change *your nappy*, change *your nappy*,**
> ***Carefully, carefully.***
> ***Throw it in the dustbin, throw it in the dustbin,***
> **Now *you're* clean, *nice and* clean!**

If you use cloth or washable nappies you could sing 'Throw it in the wash bin', 'Throw it in the bucket' or even 'Chuck it in the bucket!' if you prefer!

I am most grateful to Sing and Sign for one thing that has made our lives 1000 times easier. As soon as she could crawl, Abigail flatly refused to lie still to have her nappy changed. This was becoming a frustrating nightmare for all of us until her first week of signing classes – she learnt the sign for 'monkey' and was able to tell me that if I sang the right song (the one about the monkeys) she was happy to lie still. So, I gauge how many monkeys need to be bouncing on the bed according to how long I think it will take to change her nappy and she lies there very happily doing every single sign for that song and letting me change her nappy with no fuss at all. It really feels like a miracle!

Jane Warden

DIRTY AND CLEAN

How to sign it
DIRTY – *Rub the inside of your wrists together, just as if you have dirty cuffs. Remember to say the word 'dirty' as you do it.*

Figure 3.11 Dirty.

CLEAN – *Sweep one palm across the other upturned palm. Say 'clean'.*

Figure 3.12 Clean.

When to use it

'Dirty' and 'clean' are signs that are easy to use with the routines of changing nappies and bathtime. However, they can be great to use with any messy activity you may participate in with your child, from painting and play dough to getting muddy in the garden. For some parents, using the 'dirty' and 'clean' signs in particular can be the prelude to successfully potty training their children. Parents can begin with initially using the 'dirty' sign at the very first indication of a soiled nappy, and then on a completion of a nappy change, using the 'clean' sign. For some fortunate parents, their child picks up on these signs, and it isn't too long before he is able to communicate to them when he has a dirty nappy. Eventually, most of these children will use the 'dirty' sign as a pre-cursor to a soiled nappy – letting their parents know they need the potty. However, it is important to note, signing isn't an automatic pre-cursor to earlier potty training; it is just another way for your baby to communicate his needs to you. As with all that has been recommended so far, use as many signs as you can with your baby (only one per sentence though) and he will choose which ones are of most benefit to him.

BATH AND BED

As with mealtimes, your baby's nightly bedtime routine is a great point in the day at which to introduce some further signs to aid and encourage his vocabulary. Ideally, you are trying to create a calm, quiet, relaxed atmosphere in which you and your baby have intimate moments, whispered words and lots of hugs and kisses. Depending on your child, that may well be the reality for you on a daily basis, but if you are on baby number two, three or even four, it may well not be the case. However, the things you do that occur every night will form part of your bedtime ritual with your baby, and easily allow you to familiarize yourself with some extra signs, in context, night after night. These signs will help to give your baby the clear signal that it is time to make the transition from day to night, from activity to sleep, and that this isn't dependent on what else may be happening in the household. Nowadays most parents are told it is unnecessary to bath their baby every night, so it may not be part of your daily routine, but it is still a great occasion for your baby, and one that is normally met with squeals of delight.

BATH

How to sign it
Cross your arms over your chest and mime washing yourself. Remember to say 'bath'.

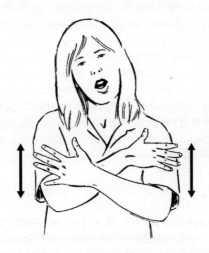

Figure 3.13 Bath.

When to use it
You can start by saying 'It's time for your *bath* (doing the sign), let's go to the bathroom.' Undoubtedly, you will be removing your baby's nappy, so don't forget to try and use the 'nappy change' sign, and maybe sing the nappy song (see page 67).

Again, just before putting your baby in the bath, you can reiterate what you are doing, saying 'You're going in the *bath* now.' Keep discussing and using the 'bath' sign as much as possible during your bathtime routine, as repetition is a key to learning for babies and children.

Most babies will love going in the bath for a splash, and this can be a great time to use many further signs with your baby, especially if you happen to fill your bath with plenty of toys. The signs for duck, boat and fish are always popular early signs for babies (see pages 78–82) so don't forget to keep using all these signs – even during bathtime.

> **REMEMBER: Repetition is the key to learning for young babies and children, so try to use as many of these signs on a daily basis as you can.**

Bedtime routines are so important; consistency will help your child to be fully aware of what is happening next and to feel more secure at bedtime. This can be especially important if you have a sensitive child who needs help adjusting to the transition from being together to being apart from you.

Now you have a nice *clean* baby all ready for bed. Does your baby go *upstairs* for bed? Maybe you give some *milk* as a last feed? Or maybe it's straight on to brushing their *teeth* or gums. Use as many signs as you can remember, and try each day to build more signs in during the bedtime rituals.

Insight

With baby number three, I don't have the same luxuries I had with my first child. The bedtime routine is often intermingled with the other children, and rarely has the continuous flow that I had with my first child. She may well be in her sleep suit 45 minutes before she actually goes to bed. However, routine is still important, as is the transition from day activity to night activity. Whether she is going down for a daytime nap or bedtime sleep, I always go to the window and 'close' the blinds, show her the 'sleep' sign, then quietly hold her next to the cot and sing the lullaby song. Just one verse is usually enough to help her make the transition and ease herself into sleep mode. Don't underestimate the importance of showing your baby these signs and keeping routines and rituals.

UPSTAIRS

How to sign it
Let your first and middle fingers of one hand make a walking movement 'up' invisible stairs.

BRUSHING TEETH

How to sign it
Very simply, with your index finger, mime brushing your front teeth.

You will find that brushing teeth is generally something babies love or hate, although for some this experience is normally just an excuse to bite the toothbrush! Why not try a simple rhyme to the tune of 'Here we go round the mulberry bush'?

> **This is the way we** brush our teeth
> **Brush our teeth**
> **Brush our teeth.**
> **This is the way we** brush our teeth
> *Before we go to bed – ed.*

TIRED

This is hardly a sign that needs explanation. It is usually obvious. This is a gesture your baby will usually do when they are tired – the rubbing of eyes is indicative that it's time for 'bed'.

How to sign it
Clench your fist and rub your eye.

When to use it
Once bathtime, nappy change and teeth cleaning have been accomplished, this might be the perfect opportunity to tell your baby that he is tired. This can easily be followed by a loud yawn using your hand to pat your mouth. Even if your baby is not tired at this point, you may well be, but still try to make your signing as

expressive as possible with different sounds and facial expressions, as your baby will respond positively to these.

So do you quietly sit in a rocking chair for a few minutes, or simply pop your baby into his cot? Maybe you read him a story first? You could ask him if he would like a book.

BOOK

How to sign it
With both hands clasped together, mime opening a book.

Many children's books will give you ample opportunity to use countless different signs you have learnt.

At this point in your nightly routine, there is no doubt that your baby knows it's time for 'bed'.

BED

How to sign it
Put your hands together on one side of your face, and then tilt your head – just as if your hands are becoming your pillow.

As you tuck your baby in, does he have something to help him settle? Maybe it's a special teddy, a favourite doll or some other comforter?

TEDDY

How to sign it
With gently clawed hands, cross your wrists across chest and tap your shoulders – almost as if you are making a cuddle gesture. Say 'teddy'.

Figure 3.14 Teddy.

DOLL

How to sign it
Hands in rocking position, but held still, saying 'doll'.

Figure 3.15 Doll.

MUSLIN

How to sign it
Make a fist, facing inwards, and rub this up and down on your cheek. Remember to say 'muslin' or whatever other word you use for their favorite comforter.

Figure 3.16 Muslin.

When to use it
This sign is great to use if your child has 'connected' with a muslin, or other piece of fabric that he regularly uses. (If it is a blanket or other such item, a top tip is to cut this into three or four squares, so you can regularly rotate and wash them. It is also not devastating for your child if it happens to get lost!)

When you begin to use these signs and label your baby's world in this way, describing with words, noise, signs and facial expressions the different routines you have, you and your baby can share a lovely conversation at bedtime about what you have done together and where you have been. Don't forget, your baby can comprehend what you are saying, and through signing can communicate his understanding to you long before he is able to talk. You may be amazed at what your baby has to share with you.

Motivating signs: animals and vehicles

Why do we call animals and vehicles 'motivating signs'? You think your baby is unlikely ever to have an urgent need to tell you he has just seen a lion in the high street? Think again. Animal pictures, animal toys and animal references make up a major part of a small baby's world. From the monkey picture on his drinking cup, to the giraffes on his curtains and the dog in his favourite book, your child sees animals everywhere. Even more exciting is that your baby loves to talk about them.

I started signing with my daughter relatively late, when she was about 13 months, after a friend introduced us to it via the Sing and Sign DVD. She picked up signs very quickly and signed them back. Her first and firm favourites for some time were cat and duck. One of the funniest occasions of her signing 'duck' early on, was when we were house hunting. We were looking at the bathroom of a house and she was signing 'duck' at us insistently. We couldn't see any ducks there – the owners were an older couple and there were no obvious signs of ducks in the bathroom, however she had spotted the light switch had a duck attached to it.

Helen Tillinghast, mum to Eloise and Joshua

Babies will often notice things that we take for granted or simply fail to notice. They will also sign for those things they hear as well as observe.

Ask any parent of a signing baby what their baby's favourite signs are and animals of all shapes and sizes will feature strongly. So here are a few to be getting on with. You can find many more on the accompanying CD-ROM.

ANIMALS

How to sign it
With palms facing down, mime 'prowling' hands going forward.

CAT

How to sign it
With both hands making 'V' shapes with the first two fingers, mime whiskers coming from your nose out. Don't forget to say 'cat'.

Figure 3.17 Cat.

DOG

How to sign it
Index and third fingers of both hands move down once in front of your chest, saying 'dog'.

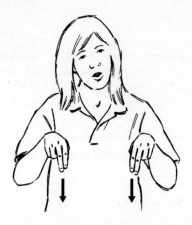

Figure 3.18 Dog.

FISH

How to sign it
Your hand faces sideways and mimes a fish tail movement 'swimming'. Remember to say 'fish'.

Figure 3.19 Fish.

You may think that you are always introducing things to your baby's world, and for a while it may feel like a one-way street. However, by signing, you are giving your child a way to express things to you and an opportunity to 'tell' you what is important in his world, long before he can verbalize it.

BIRD

How to sign it
With your thumb and index finger of one hand, open and close several times (keep the other three fingers clenched) – as if you were doing a mime for opening and closing a bird's beak.

BEE

How to sign it
Again with your thumb and index finger together, make random loops in the air. Great with a good 'bzzzzzzz' sound too!

DUCK

How to sign it
This is a sign you may naturally do with your baby. Open and close your whole hand as if it were a beak making a 'quacking' move.

ELEPHANT

How to sign it
Make a fist, take it up to your nose and mime a big trunk, with a little flourish at the end.

CROCODILE

How to sign it
Think of your hands and arms as the jaws of a croc, and with both hands mime a big snapping action.

CHICKEN

How to sign it
Your elbows become wings, so move them in and out, like a chicken.

MONKEY

How to sign it
For this one, there is nothing for it but to look like a monkey, so with both arms stretched out horizontally, bend them at the elbow and start scratching under your arms!

RABBIT

How to sign it
With your index and middle fingers make 'rabbit ears' on your head, and twitch them forward slightly.

SHEEP

How to sign it
With your little fingers, mime curly horns coming out from your temples.

Animal and vehicle signs are not only great fun, they also encourage your baby to play around with the sounds that are the building blocks of future speech. You may not be keen to call a 'sheep' a 'baa baa' or to call an 'aeroplane' a 'neeowww', but sounds such as these are wonderful practice for those little mouths getting around the speech sounds they will soon be using. We will cover speech sounds in more detail in Chapter 7.

> **REMEMBER: Your child will want to tell you about things in his world that interest him – whether they be visual or audible.** It may well be things that as adults we take for granted or just no longer see or hear. Children are often more perceptive and as the old saying goes, try to 'see things through a child's eyes'.

If animals aren't a firm favourite with your child, then you may find that vehicles captivate his attention. Boys in particular seem to love anything that moves or has wheels, often feeling the need to find out how they work. So if you find your child is fascinated by moving parts – bikes, cars, trains, etc. – then the following signs are ones you might find particularly helpful.

TRAIN

How to sign it
With arms bent and fists clenched at your sides, mime train wheels and say 'train'.

Figure 3.20 Train.

Insight

'Train' was a relatively early one my first son picked up on. He was around a year old when we moved to a new house. Every breakfast he would sit in the kitchen and sign 'train'. I hunted high and low for a train – looking for train magnets on the fridge, stickers, or just a lost train that hadn't found its way back to the toy box. Nothing. I told him I couldn't see a train, and signed 'where'. For a while he just kept signing train. Then one day, he put his hand up to his ear and signed 'train'. Of course! He could 'hear' the trains – I hadn't registered the low rumble of the trains – we were at least a mile or two away from the nearest railway line.

CAR

How to sign it
With hands in front of you, mime a small steering wheel.

BOAT

How to sign it
Touch your fingertips together, palms facing inwards but apart, so you are making a boat's 'bow' shape. Move your boat shape forward, saying 'boat'.

Figure 3.21 Boat.

AEROPLANE

How to sign it
Make a fist and then have your thumb and little finger sticking out as if they are wings. You can then move your 'plane' through the sky, making the appropriate 'neeeoooooowwww' sound!

When Helen and her daughter were playing out in the garden, Eloise spotted an aeroplane and so her mum naturally signed 'plane' to her – then a bird flew by and Eloise signed 'bird' to her mum, then when she realized nothing else was flying by she signed and said 'more'. Helen found it hilarious that

More useful signs

So far we have covered some early basic signs that you can use many times in a day and will give you lots of practice in signing with your baby. We have also covered signs that babies find motivating and are often among the first signs they will use. We will now progress on to some signs that you as a parent or carer might find really helpful when communicating with your child. These are some of the most common signs parents will ask for. It is worth noting, at this point, that these are generally not signs babies will tend to use early on, as they are not as motivating for them as going on the 'swings' or watching the 'trains'. However, you will be amazed at how many babies from one year onwards will use some or all of these signs.

When your baby gets a little more active, their modest world suddenly opens up. From being a small baby who will sit and play beautifully with a selection of toys, suddenly he is able to crawl or maybe bottom shuffle and then walk. Favourite ornaments are hastily removed, certain cupboard doors may be child-proofed (and sometimes adult-proofed!) and, for some, this is when the grey hairs begin to appear as you try to maintain a safe and yet stimulating environment for your baby.

Before we even had Sasha, my husband began to worry about having a baby in the house with his precious speakers. Since Sasha started crawling, the 'no' sign has been invaluable, especially regarding Daddy's speakers and other gadgets. She will crawl up to them and then sign 'no' and now says 'no, no, no' at the same time. She knows exactly what she can and can't touch and we don't need to keep repeating ourselves.

Angie Duckett

If your child is heading towards or reaching out to touch something hazardous, or is putting himself into a potentially dangerous situation, you may wish to continue to use the 'stop', or 'no' sign, each of which would be equally valid. However, as you are aware, it is so important to immerse children in language, and as he gets older you may wish to use different words and signs, while keeping the message the same. 'Dangerous' can provide a great alternative to the 'stop' or 'no' sign.

DANGEROUS

How to sign it
Start with your index finger touching between your eyes. Use a straight hand, facing sideways and move down strongly in an arc. Remember to say 'dangerous'.

Figure 3.22 Dangerous.

When to use it
As your baby gets older and begins walking, you can use the 'dangerous' sign many times during the day. When outside you can use this sign near the roads, in conjunction with the 'wait' and 'stop' signs, or indeed as you beckon to them to 'come away'.

As parents with young children, we aim to provide a safe home environment for them; however, you may find your family's and friends' houses are not quite so baby friendly. Anything electrical or mechanical seems to hold a special fascination, and for some the fireplace also seems a great place to explore. The 'dangerous' sign might be one that becomes extremely evident within your signing vocabulary, and don't forget it will often be used in conjunction with the 'no' or 'don't touch' signs too.

HOT

As you can imagine, 'hot' is a particularly useful sign for your young baby to learn, and again is often used in conjunction with the 'don't touch', 'no' or even 'dangerous' signs – all of which we have previously covered. 'Hot' is such an easy sign to learn and use, and it's very expressive too.

How to sign it
With five fingers spread apart, quickly touch your fingers to your lips and then withdraw them – saying 'hot'.

Figure 3.23 Hot.

Will had been using signs at home but he hadn't really used them around people he didn't know. Shortly after Will's first birthday we were at a restaurant for a family meal. He crawled over to a bar area that had spot lights mounted into a foot rest, he pulled himself up to stand near a light, he turned round and signed 'hot' to the waitress! I couldn't believe it. He was getting more and more confident every day. I told the waitress what he was saying and she was amazed. This baby knew the lights were hot and he told us even though he couldn't talk.

Kathryn Furber

When to use it

To try to help your child learn and understand the concept of 'hot' you may wish to use a recently finished hot drink and gently place their hand on the edge of the warm cup and sign 'hot'. You can follow this with the 'don't touch' ('no') sign.

> **WARNING: Although your baby may understand the concept of 'hot' please continue to ensure that hot drinks and any other hot objects are well away from baby's reach or otherwise protected.**

Another time to use the 'hot' sign is during dinner, especially if you are waiting for your child's dinner to cool down. If this is the case, let your child know his dinner is 'hot' – again you may wish to carefully place his hand on the side of the bowl, and sign 'hot'. You may then wish to let your child know that he needs to 'wait', using the 'wait' sign (holding both hands in the air, as if you are saying 'stop' – see page 113 for a full description). This will not only help your child to grasp the concept of why he needs to wait for his dinner, it will also help him comprehend the concept of what the word 'hot' means.

When your child can sign these important messages to you, you will finally realize that he comprehends what you are saying, and by using signing, he can communicate his understanding to you. Bear in mind your baby can be signing these concepts long before he is talking.

Mariette and I have been signing since she was 11 months old. We joined a signing class to help us to learn and to have some fun socializing too. Mariette very quickly learnt the 'hot' sign (very handy for obvious reasons) and 'finished', which was brilliant as it stopped her from throwing her food bowl across the room when she didn't want to eat any more! Also from a safety point of view, for example, 'stop', 'hot' and 'pain' were all really useful signs. We have found signing invaluable as it has lowered the number of tantrums she was having!

Elizabeth Nurse

COLD

How to sign it
Clench your fists directly in front of your chest, then in small movements shake them up and down, as if you were miming a 'brrrr!'

When to use it
Working along the same lines as 'hot', an easy way to introduce the 'cold' sign to your baby is with a pack of frozen peas carefully wrapped in a tea towel. By placing his hand briefly on the cold peas, you can make the word 'cold' go from an obscure word to an understandable concept. For example, if you have a child who doesn't like to put his coat on, by helping him to understand the reason why it is important – because it's cold outside – you are hopefully a little closer to your child wanting to do it more willingly. You may be surprised that sometimes just a quick explanation can be all the incentive a child needs.

My daughter Gabrielle would sign to me at bedtime whether her milk was too hot or cold, enabling me to settle her very quickly.

Michelle Elmer

It is amazing at how quickly babies can understand a particular sign, and transfer that knowledge into different situations and scenarios. I can remember one parent telling me she had entered her daughter's bedroom in the night as she was crying. After checking her daughter's nappy, and making sure she wasn't thirsty, she asked her daughter what the matter was. Her daughter signed 'cold'. She had only taught her the sign two weeks previously.

By giving your baby a whole range of signs relevant to his world, you are giving him many opportunities to communicate in ways that you may not have thought possible. Included throughout this book are real-life illustrations of situations where parents have used the various signs described. This is done in the hope that it will inspire you to use as many signs as you can remember with your child. Nevertheless, don't get too carried away with your signing and forget the golden rule of only signing one word per sentence to your child.

NAUGHTY

How to sign it
With a clenched fist in front of you, raise your little finger.

When to use it
At this point it is worth noting the importance of labelling your child's behaviour as naughty, rather than labelling your child as naughty. For example, 'Don't throw your food on the floor – that's naughty' would be a way to label the behaviour, or you may wish to limit it further and just say 'No, naughty', rather than use an inappropriate phrase such as 'You naughty boy'.

GENTLE

Gentle describes a way of behaving that we would all wish our children to display around others, and especially younger babies. It seems that some children right from birth are naturally soft and gentle, and continue throughout their lives to be so. However, it appears that the majority of children go through a stage, usually around the age of two, of being less than gentle with younger babies, animals, etc. Some have a natural, almost idle curiosity, and so, on occasion, want to find out what does happen when you pull at the little baby, or yank the cat's tail.

The sign to use for 'gentle' is a great sign and is one that is very effective whether you are right next to your child or, if they are more familiar with it, from across the other side of a room. It is a very expressive sign, and when you use it you may find that your voice softens, and naturally becomes lower and slower.

How to sign it
With one hand, slowly and gently stroke the back of your other hand, remembering to say the word 'gentle' at the same time.

Figure 3.24 Gentle.

When to use it
'Gentle' is quite a difficult concept to explain to a child and can often be misunderstood. One of the reasons why a child can misunderstand the word is because we, as adults, tend to use it when our children are actually being rough – so, when our child tugging at another child, we will say 'be gentle'. This can give mixed messages if the child hasn't fully understood what 'gentle' means.

One way to avoid the above scenario and give your child the correct meaning for the word 'gentle', is to take his hand and gently stroke a baby's hand, arm, leg or tummy, while saying 'gentle' – you can then proceed to show him the sign. As much as possible it is better to use the word in a positive context like this, before using it to indicate the behaviour that you would like to see if he is being too rough.

WHAT

This is a sign that you may find you begin to use quite a lot –
'*What* is it?', '*What* do you want?' How many times is your baby
crying, pointing, trying to talk or doing something that you don't
understand? All children go through the baby babble stage. They
are trying to make sense of their world and relating it to us in
'baby talk'. Often we are totally ignorant of 'conversations' they
are engaging in with us. The frustration for some babies is very
apparent. Signing at least gives your child the opportunity to tell
you what the problem is.

How to sign it
Wave your index finger from side to side.

When to use it
Next time your child is trying to 'tell' you something, demanding
that you understand, why not try using the 'what' sign? You may
find that this stops your child in their tracks (especially if they are
crying). Your child will know they are getting your attention and it
provides him with the opportunity to 'tell' you what the problem is.

When asking '*What* do you want?', you may wish to give some
prompts, such as 'Would you like a *drink*?', using the sign and, if
their drink is handy, holding that up too. If that clearly isn't the
answer, you can sign 'no' and try something else. Once you know
what it is your child is after, don't forget to show him the sign, and
say the word. It won't be long before your child learns the signs for
the things that are important to him, which will limit the times you
have to guess what it is he wants.

LOOK

On the surface you may think this is a sign you won't use very
often, but you may be surprised at how incredibly useful it can be.

How to sign it
*Point your index finger towards your eye and then swiftly move it away
in the direction of where you are indicating to your child to look.*

When to use it

The most obvious scenarios for using this sign are when you are trying to show your child a new object, or to gain their attention, to look at a bird in the tree, for example. When you want your child to maintain eye contact with you, it is also useful to use this sign. Some children find keeping eye contact easier than others – but it is vital when giving an instruction, or when telling your child how much you love him. Keep aiming for good eye contact, and use the 'look' sign.

NOW

This may not be a sign that you use when you are beginning to sign with a young baby, but is extremely useful with a toddler, especially one who has a strong will! 'Now' is a great sign that lets your hands do the talking for you, and the sharp movement helps communicate the urgency of what you are requiring.

How to sign it
Start with your palms facing upwards and your fingertips facing in at chest level, then make one strong movement down to waist level. Remember to say 'now'.

Figure 3.25 Now.

When to use it
I have noticed parents using this sign across the playground with primary-aged children, asking their child to come 'now' – again letting their hands rather than their voice do the shouting.

QUICK/HURRY UP

How to sign it
Use one index finger to quickly strike the side of the other index finger.

When to use it
This is another sign that goes hand in hand with the 'now' sign, and is used in similar circumstances. You can also use this sign to play games with your child, alternating between quick and slow.

CAREFUL

How to sign it
With your thumb and index finger, form the letter 'C'. Move two 'C'-shaped hands down and out from your eyes, while saying 'careful'.

Figure 3.26 Careful.

When to use it
'Careful' is a valuable sign that you can use in a variety of circumstances. You may find you use it with early walkers, or boisterous boys who love to climb, or even a young child holding a pet or a new baby. You will find this often goes hand in hand with the 'gentle' sign shown on page 89.

PLAY/TOYS

How to sign it
With flat hands, make small upward moving circles in front of you, rotating your wrists and saying 'play'.

Figure 3.27 Play/toys.

When to use it
You can use this any time you reach for the toy box at home. Alternatively you may wish to use this sign when you go to playgroup or a parent and toddler environment to signify going to play with the toys.

Insight
Through signing your baby can comprehend what you are saying, and, in turn, can communicate his understanding to you long before he is able to talk.

At this point in the book you should have a good understanding of what baby signing is and how to incorporate some of the signs into your daily life. Many of the routines you and your baby will go through each day have been covered, with many additional motivating signs included to enable you to show your baby the signs for things that relate directly to his world.

10 THINGS TO REMEMBER

1 Mealtime is a great time of day to try using all the first basic signs.

2 'Where' is a great first sign to introduce to other family members. It's easy, and many a game can be initiated using this simple sign.

3 'Open' is a sign that can be used with many routines in your day – everything from opening the curtains after nap time, a bag of toys or maybe a yoghurt pot at feed time. This is a good motivating sign for babies, particularly as it brings about immediate results.

4 When you are preparing to go out, remember a few signs to help your child prepare, such as those for their shoes or coat. Don't forget to tell him where you are headed!

5 If your child struggles when it's time to put on his shoes, or maybe have his nappy changed, try singing to him. Doing things rhythmically seems to calm babies – plus it's good for their brain development.

6 Once you have mastered the basic signs at mealtimes, try adding the 'dirty' and 'clean' signs.

7 Routine is important for children. They love to know what's coming up next. Nap time is especially important as they make that transition from activity to sleep. Try using a few signs to prepare your baby for bed. Stopping by his cot and singing a simple lullaby can help ease that transition time.

8 Find out what motivates your child – what is it that gets him excited? For some, it's food, for others, it might be animals or vehicles that set their arms flapping and elicit excited squeals. Try to provide your child with more of these motivating signs.

9 *Children love to explore and can often get themselves into tight spots. 'Dangerous' or 'don't touch/no' may well become frequently used signs in your repertoire. Try using these signs in conjunction with beckoning to your child to 'come away'.*

10 *'Careful' and 'gentle' are signs that are often used together. When you first introduce the 'gentle' sign, try to use it to show gentleness, rather than using it at a point when your child is being rough. Using the sign to ask your child to be gentle could initially suggest the wrong meaning of the sign.*

4

Emotional development

In this chapter you will learn:
- *the importance of labelling your child's emotions*
- *signs to use to help your child's emotional development.*

Emotions – how does your baby feel?

Signs for feelings are very valuable for babies, although hugely
underestimated. Fortunately for parents, emotions are easily
revealed to parents of young babies; they don't ever try to hide them
as we might as adults. They are open books in that respect, and we
can read them well. When they are tired they often begin by rubbing
their eyes, or yawning – catching these cues early, you can easily
show your baby the appropriate sign, and then put her straight down
for a sleep. Missing that early cue often results in a crying baby who
can be much harder to settle. When they are happy or find something
or someone funny, they will naturally begin laughing. However, if
they are angry, sad, tired, frightened or in pain, they may cry and
you may not be sure which emotion they are expressing. Emotional
development is often seriously understated when dealing with babies
and toddlers, despite it being a primary feature in their lives. Much
of a baby's world revolves around her emotions.

> Anna told me her daughter was 16 months old when she saw
> her friend in a stripy black and white jumper. Her daughter
> immediately started laughing, and signing 'zebra'!

The above is such a wonderful example of how we can see a baby's or toddler's personality and sense of humour developing and, through signing, give her a great opportunity to share it with us. No longer are you left to guess the source of your child's pleasure. When she can point and sign the source of her amusement – a 'zebra' sign on observing a stripy jumper, for example – you will enjoy a mutually rewarding exchange.

Insight

Emotions are such a powerful thing for young babies – they are, after all, what drive them and they have no other way of communicating. Some children are naturally easy and laid-back, while others are more emotional or 'highly strung'. Whatever the temperament of your child, using the signs for various emotions can be surprisingly effective.

HAPPY

How to sign it
Keep left cupped hand still, then rub right cupped hand from index finder out to thumb. Rub cupped hands with glee.

Figure 4.1 Happy.

SAD

How to sign it
Move a flat hand (facing sideways, fingertips up) down the middle of your face.

> **Insight**
> When your baby is angry, sad, tired or frightened, try showing empathy and understanding by labelling such emotions with signs. Offering labels in this way can comfort those feelings beyond your baby's control and lead to supporting benefits in emotional development.

LAUGH/FUNNY

How to sign it
Make a 'C' with index finger and thumb, and move it up and down in front of your jaw, as if you are miming the jaw moving up and down with laughter.

TIRED

How to sign it
A really natural sign – with a clenched fist, rub your eye.

FRIGHTENED

How to sign it
Clawed hand trembles in front of your chest.

When to use it
It can be the strangest things – which may seem quite bizarre to us – that frighten children. Many children, for example, are frightened by clowns, or people dressed up in large animal suits. Numerous images on the television can be too much for your young child to comprehend. Your child will not know or be able to verbalize this strange feeling within. However, she will know that she desperately needs the comfort and safety of Mum or Dad.

You can use this opportunity to show your child the frightened sign as described above and, where appropriate, gently show your child the frightening object – indicating that it is not something she needs to be fearful of.

ANGRY

How to sign it
Clawed hands, with palms facing you, make small movements alternating up and down.

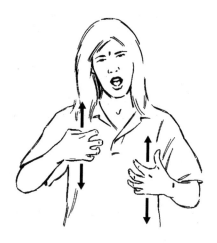

Figure 4.2 Angry.

For many adults, labelling feelings seems a strange concept, and an area that can provoke a few questions: Do I really want to show my child the angry sign, when I want her to be calm and loving? Will showing her such signs not make my child angrier?

You will be showing your child these signs in context, so therefore your child will already be feeling these emotions, but may not necessarily understand the depth or breadth of emotions within. By giving your child a sign for these emotions, you are also showing a deep level of understanding. Therefore this range of signs can help babies cope with strong emotions and feel understood.

Toddlers who are familiar with the 'angry' sign will often use it themselves to channel their frustration. It is a very descriptive sign for how your baby is feeling when she has 'lost it'. Many two-year-olds who signed as babies still use this sign to show frustration when deeply upset. It is far better to use such a sign than thrashing out, and gives them an appropriate way to show their anger. This is a sign that can be useful even when your child is able to say the word, as it is such a descriptive sign.

WHY DOES MY CHILD OFTEN SEEM FRUSTRATED?

Pre-verbal children are often frustrated as a result of not being understood, and therefore their needs not being met. Parents of signing children often comment that signing has reduced frustration and temper tantrums in their children. In some children, signing has proven to almost eliminate tantrums completely! And it has been reported that those who still succumb to them do so as a result of being told 'no' rather than from the frustration of not being understood. Unfortunately, we will always be setting boundaries for our children, so for those stronger-willed children, signing can play a significant role, but those tantrums, although reduced, may continue when limits are set and enforced.

I have observed some babies who really thought they could talk, although we adults could only hear double Dutch.
These children can get very frustrated when they are urgently trying to tell you something. They may repeat their utterance twice or maybe three times, almost begging you to understand their baby babble. On these occasions, I would suggest that you give your child good eye contact, and ask her to sign it to you as well. Then you should finally be able to understand what she is trying to communicate. Each time this happens, try to use the opportunity to reiterate the word she has been so desperately trying to form. Get her to copy it and repeat it back to you if you can. In the early stages it is likely to be far from perfect and intelligible, but next time at least you may have an idea what 'bogahhhdaaaa' is!

Included below is a case study of a mum and her son who often appeared angry and frustrated. You will notice how Jane, the mum, appropriately uses the 'angry' sign with her strong-willed son. This will hopefully give you more insight into the effect that labelling feelings can have on your child.

Case study

As Jayden was quite poorly from a very young age, he had to undergo numerous tests – at just two weeks old he had to have a lumbar puncture. From an early age, with constant admissions to hospital, his experience was that people hurt him, things and food that went in his mouth hurt him, etc. He always seemed a bit 'different' from other children. He certainly wasn't very social, and was often tetchy and angry. When he was about a year old, I can remember thinking, my goodness, if my son is like this at one, what on earth will he be like at two? (The terrible twos by then was an alarming thought, with a wild one-year-old!) He is a strong-willed boy, but then that's hardly surprising as quite a few times he has had to fight for his very existence. Although we were aware of what he had gone through, and this had given a little justification for how he was, it still wasn't much comfort when

(Contd)

your 13-month-old was having a huge tantrum! It was then that we began to use more of the feelings signs we had been taught, especially the 'angry' sign. It was incredible. When we started to give him a label for his feelings, and show him we understood what he was experiencing, he really calmed down. I was able to empathize, and let him know I understood he was angry (even though I didn't always understand why). It was as if by recognizing and acknowledging his feelings he felt as if he didn't need to fight so hard, and he would then often soften towards me, and allow me to comfort him. I cannot tell you what a breakthrough that was for us as a family.

Jane and Jayden

Singing is a great way of releasing emotion and expressing yourself. Try singing this to the tune of 'If you're happy and you know it', it's great for teaching your child about emotions.

If you're angry *and you know it stamp your feet!*
If you're angry *and you know it stamp your feet!*
If you're angry *and you know it*
and you really want to show it
If you're angry *and you know it stamp your feet.*

Other verses can include:

▶ *If you're naughty and you know it say you're sorry.*
▶ *If you're tired and you know it go to sleep.*
▶ *If you're sad and you know it have a cry.*
▶ *If you're frightened and you know it have a cuddle.*

The list can continue as long as your imagination allows.

Insight

Music can play a very important role in your child's life, and as we have already learnt, it is good for their brain development. You may like to try experimenting with different styles and types of music – from quiet lullaby sounds to some harsher classical pieces. You can lie still with the quiet pieces of music, and move around with the louder ones – incorporating many of the emotion signs, as well as signs for 'loud' and 'quiet', during active listening times.

Pain and medicine

'Pain' may not be a sign you may initially think of using with a baby, unless of course they have particular health issues. However, think of a six-month-old trying to sit up for the first time who keeps falling over; a nine-month-old standing, holding on to furniture and losing their balance; a 13-month-old taking their first steps before becoming unsteady on their feet; an 18-month-old who is trying out stairs for the first time; a two-year-old who is running too fast – these are just simple everyday occurrences in your child's life where the 'pain' sign can easily be implemented.

Insight
Do try to implement this important sign – you never know when it might be invaluable for you, as some of the examples in this section show. If your child has bumped her knee, then use the sign next to their knee. Your child will soon learn how to sign which part of her body is hurt.

PAIN/HURT

How to sign it
Point both index fingers towards each other and keep prodding them together.

Figure 4.3 Pain.

When to use it
Somewhere around the age of six months, a baby's first two lower front teeth will begin to poke through her gums – for most children this will cause varying degrees of pain and discomfort. If you suspect that this is the reason why your baby is fussing or crying, use the 'pain' sign, near the mouth or gum area. For some babies, a more concrete and immediate use of the sign is beneficial, so also use the pain sign anytime your baby falls over and bumps herself.

You never know how showing your baby these useful signs will impact on your family, or indeed how your child may come to use them, as Martin discovered with his eldest son.

Case study

I thought learning to use the pain and feeling signs was a little odd for such young babies, but didn't realize how useful these would become. I had been told how to use the pain sign, and initially began using it whenever he fell over and bumped himself. A few months after learning them, I put my son to bed, and he began crying. I went in, said 'ssshhhh, ssshh', told him to go to sleep and went out again. He continued crying. I went back in again after a few minutes, checked his nappy, made sure he wasn't too hot, etc., settled him down again, and left the room. The third time, I just lay him down again and walked out (I knew he wasn't hungry as he had recently had his milk). I couldn't perceive any reason for the crying – I wanted him to know I was still around, but I also wanted him to know this was the time for him to sleep. The fifth time of going in and out, I turned to him and said '*What* is it? *What's* the matter?' (signing 'what'). Of course, I didn't expect any response from him, after all he couldn't talk... He sat there crying and then signed 'pain'. I was astounded. It would never have entered my head that his continual crying was because he was in pain. I had just thought he didn't want to go to sleep, and was protesting about being put in his bed. My natural instinct if the crying had continued would be to sit next to his cot, as a presence for him, until he settled. Giving him medicine wouldn't have occurred to me as it wasn't the high-pitched pain cry he had when he fell over, etc. I couldn't believe I would never have known he was in pain, if he wasn't able to sign to me. I immediately picked him up, cuddled him and gave him Calpol. Within half an hour he had settled.

After this 'successful' attempt at using this sign, we found he was using it more regularly, often a little while after dinner. It later transpired he had food allergies and was even intolerant to the soya milk the hospital had given him. Even now, if he has foods he is allergic to, he will get stomach cramps, diarrhoea, etc., but initially we had no idea he was experiencing all this as a baby, too. It is at times like this that signing has been invaluable for us as a family, allowing us to appropriately respond to our children, and giving them a way to effectively communicate with us.

Martin

Try signing 'pain' whenever your baby bumps or hurts herself this week. Many babies respond very well to this sign and can begin to use it appropriately themselves. Teething is something that every baby goes through with varying degrees of distress. Jess was a very bright little girl and at around 15 months old was frequently putting a few signs together – signing in sentences. She would often sign 'pain' to her mum, Joanne, point to her teeth, then 'medicine' and 'more' – an incredibly clear indication of what she needed to alleviate her discomfort.

Top tip

When using the 'pain' sign with your child, use it to indicate the area that is hurting, for example, knee, tummy or teeth. When your child uses it for herself, she can show you what or where in her body is hurting.

MEDICINE

How to sign it
Make a loosely held fist with your left hand, then with the little fingertip of your right hand trace around the top of the fist – as if tracing the opening of a small jar.

Figure 4.4 Medicine.

When to use it
Whenever your child requires medication, try to use this sign before you administer the medicine.

DOCTOR

How to sign it
With thumb underneath and index finger on top, place on edge of wrist (as if taking a pulse).

When to use it
It is best to wait until you are outside the doctors' surgery before using this sign for the first time, otherwise it will be an abstract concept to your child, or a sign that could get easily confused with something else. If you are feeling brave and not too distracted, you may like to use it again during your consultation. Some babies will end up making frequent visits to the doctor or hospital, so this sign may become useful before setting out on the journey. For other babies it won't feature in their repertoire of signs they use.

The parents of most non-signing babies can only begin to guess at what may be causing their baby to be unsettled. With signing babies we have so much more understanding and can make educated guesses at what the positive benefits are to our child when they have the ability to communicate and be fully understood. The expectation is that it can only impact positively on their confidence, self-esteem and emotional development.

Tahlia's first signs were 'where' and 'hurt' (she had to go to hospital for five weeks for surgery when she was one year old and has since had several medical treatments). She then quickly progressed to 'Mummy' (using one instead of three fingers), 'no' (which she also uses for 'finished'), 'change nappy' (also pointing to her bum!) and 'butterfly'. She is now 18 months old and in the last few weeks we've seen an explosion of signs from Tahlia. It's as though she's slowly been absorbing them and is now ready to talk fluently with her hands as well as her voice – albeit still in her own language most of the time! We can tell she gets a lot of satisfaction from the fact that we understand her so much better,
(Contd)

and praise her so much when she signs and speaks. Interestingly she doesn't sign much in class or when she watches the Sing and Sign DVD, but does more and more the rest of the time.

Alison Lovegrove

Love and manners

'I love you' is a wonderful sign to share, either as three separate signs or just as the single 'love' sign, which is simpler for younger babies to grasp.

LOVE

How to sign it
Two hands cross lovingly across your chest.

When to use it
This sign in particular is one that can last for years, and can be great to use across a crowded room.

Insight
This sign was always a firm favourite and was frequently followed by hugs and kisses. It still features strongly in our family as a sign – often given to the boys in a chance glance from some distance away, when using words just wouldn't be appropriate, or would embarrass them too much!

PLEASE

How to sign it
With a flat hand on your chin, fingertips pointing up, palm towards you, move your hand out and down from your chin in a large arc.

Figure 4.5 Please.

When to use it

When you are just setting out with signing, and your baby may only be around six months old, the signs for 'please' and 'thank you' aren't ones to place too heavy an importance on, as these tend to be words that delight parents, rather than words that make babies happy. Early signs therefore should be words that babies really want to say. Inspiring communication is so much more fun than requesting it.

Insight

Occasionally, parents have come to me complaining that their child is not signing. They inform me they have started with please and thank you (and maybe one or two more signs) and have been 100 per cent consistent. They feel that signing is not working for them. They have failed to realize that please and thank you are parent-pleasing signs and not child-inspiring signs. I strongly believe that every parent should teach these signs, but not to the exclusion of others that will be far more inspiring to their child.

Conversely, slightly older babies are more prepared for the niceties of manners and politeness and therefore 'please' and 'thank you' begin to be attractive signs to encourage and use more and more in your daily signing. It isn't too long before babies realize that saying 'please' will achieve a positive result. Most parents are delighted when their child learns the art of good manners before being able to speak.

Top tip

Parents can sometimes get confused between the 'please' and 'thank you' signs as one is a longer gesture of the other. When signing 'please', think 'please to your knees' as it is a larger gesture than 'thank you', which remains quite short and static.

THANK YOU

How to sign it
With a flat hand on your chin, fingertips pointing up, palm towards you, move your fingertips out and down from your chin in a small static movement that should finish about 10–15 cm (4–6 in) from your face.

Figure 4.6 Thank you.

When to use it
When teaching a child to be appreciative, some parents will start with trying to get their child to say 'ta' while others will only use

'thank you'. This is a purely individual choice and the sign will remain the same even if you progress from 'ta' to 'thank you'. Babies find 'ta' an easier word to say, while 'thank you' babies will tend to mimic the intonation in your voice rather than repeating the actual word. Both can be pleasing to parents, especially when accompanied by the sign.

Insight

Continue to use the 'thank you' sign with your child even when they are able to say the word. You will find there will be many occasions when even a primary-school-aged child will forget to say 'thank you'. You can silently prompt them with the 'thank you' sign, and make your child appear to have excellent manners.

SORRY

Even if your baby is starting to talk, there are likely to be some favourite signs that stay around for a while. Some signs are particularly recommended to continue using, even if your baby is saying the word. 'Sorry' is one such word.

How to sign it
Make a fist, and rub a small circle in the middle of your chest.

Figure 4.7 Sorry.

When to use it

Sometimes babies are too ashamed (or even too proud!) to say the word, so rather than have a stand-off, which can end up being distressing for everyone, the sorry sign can offer a shy apology. You can also use this gesture to prompt your child to say sorry.

Insight

During class one day a little girl grabbed an instrument off a stunned little boy. The mum told (and signed) to her daughter that was 'naughty' and she needed to give it back. On seeing the 'naughty' sign the little girl began to sign 'sorry' and immediately smothered the surprised little boy in hugs and kisses.

SHARE

All of us want our children to be caring, sharing individuals who are ready and willing to share their toys. The reality is that many children, especially toddlers, become very territorial and some, just for a short time, can become unwilling to relinquish or share property. This is largely due to a young child not being able to understand the idea that something given up now can be retrieved later. Also patience is in short supply at this age.

How to sign it
Mime 'give' and 'take' with both hands, palms facing upwards.

Figure 4.8 Share.

When to use it
You will have many opportunities to use this sign among friends, at mother and toddler groups or with siblings. It is a powerful sign that accurately describes what is involved.

Insight

Most children perceive sharing as having to surrender a favourite toy or possession. One way to turn this on its head is to make sharing an enjoyable experience by using, for example, a favourite food. If you give your child a snack of bread while you are eating their favourite food, it is highly likely they will point, grab or do anything to get their favourite food from your plate. You can use this opportunity to show the 'share' sign, maybe saying a phrase such as 'Mummy *share* her strawberries with you?' This also works well when turned into a game with a favourite toy, teaching your child to take turns and 'share'. Giving your child this opportunity to share in a non-threatening environment enables you to judge the time to 'share' it back again. Learning in this way gives your child a head start when it comes to sharing with friends of her own age.

WAIT

How to sign it
Put both hands in front of your body, hands flat, palms outwards, then move your hands purposefully down in front of you.

Figure 4.9 Wait.

When to use it

This can be an incredibly useful sign in a variety of circumstances – a child pulling at your leg when you are paying for goods, waiting to cross the road, or desperate for food that is cooling.

Insight

As your child gets older and wants to interrupt you, you can allow your hands to do the talking, asking her to wait until you are finished. 'Wait' is a very simple sign that holds a strong message.

By using the signs for emotions, signs for when your child is in pain or discomfort, as well as those all-important signs associated with manners, you will be able to engage with your child on a level that simply was not possible before. You will be able to enter her world, one that is filled with emotions, and begin to show empathy with her by labelling her emotions with signs or by acknowledging her pain. The benefits of using these signs cannot be underestimated.

TEST YOUR KNOWLEDGE

1 *Why are emotions and feelings so important for babies?*

2 *Before you read this book, how did your baby communicate feelings (such as tiredness) to you?*

3 *In a baby's world, what is one of the aspects of communication that revolves around them?*

4 *Signs such as 'sad', 'laugh', 'tired' and 'frightened' help a baby to cope with what?*

5 *What might be the outcome of not understanding or meeting the needs of a pre-verbal child?*

6 *What positive expectations and benefits might we see in babies that have been introduced to baby signing compared to those that haven't?*

7 *What point in your baby's development is a good time to introduce the 'pain' sign. How should it be introduced?*

8 *Why is it not necessary to place too much importance on signs such as 'please' and 'thank you' with a young baby?*

9 *What is a common perception among children when asked to share something they own? In what practical ways can you help to change this?*

10 *Why is 'wait' an important sign to teach in terms of your child's development?*

See answer section at the back of the book.

5

Encouraging signing with
children at home and
in childcare

In this chapter you will learn:
- *creative ways to sign for important people in your life*
- *how to maintain signing if your child is at nursery or in daycare*
- *about effective communication with a child in a bilingual family.*

Important people in your baby's world

By using signs for the names of favourite friends and relatives, you can enrich your baby's excitement and anticipation at seeing them. You can choose from the signs listed here or you can be inventive, creating gestures that indicate personal characteristics such as glasses or a beard – maybe you have a family member who is particularly clever, the sign for which is dragging a thumb horizontally across your forehead – or you could use the sign for an initial letter of a person's name (see the alphabet on the Sing and Sign CD-ROM). Your baby will not yet have the fine motor control to form some letter shapes accurately but this does not matter. Be accurate yourself and let your baby approximate at this stage.

MUMMY

How to sign it
Index, middle and ring fingers tap twice on the opposite palm.

DADDY

How to sign it
With closed index and middle finger, tap twice on the closed index and middle finger of the opposite hand.

Insight

Signing can help to make coming home time for mummy or daddy a major event in your household. A quick text saying that you are two minutes away can ensure that baby is told to watch and 'wait' at the window. Rattling keys, the sound of the garage door or whistling up the path can be the signal to sign 'listen'… and then 'mummy' or 'daddy'. It's fantastic to be greeted by hugs and kisses as you enter the door, and can be a time of great excitement for your baby.

Don't forget those oh-so-motivating characters such as Noddy, the Teletubbies and the Fimbles. Remember to consider what your baby wants to talk about and what is important in his world. Be imaginative in creating signs for your baby.

Baby signing is wonderful fun for all the family, and older siblings love it. They often master signs quickly and adore this 'special' communication with their little brother or sister. Around five to six months of age you will notice your baby is begin to show much more recognition with significant family members, so these can be great early signs to show your baby.

BROTHER

How to sign it
*Make a fist, with thumbs up, knuckles inwards, and rub up
and down.*

Figure 5.1 Brother.

SISTER

How to sign it
Hooked index finger taps the bridge of your nose twice.

When to use it
If your baby has an older brother or sister, you can use these signs
any time you use his or her name. However, if he has more than
one brother or more than one sister, you will have to be inventive,
and create a sign for additional siblings – maybe one loves to
sing, so you could mime a microphone in front of your mouth, or
another has long hair, so you could mime that. Alternatively, you
may like to use the 'boy' and 'girl' signs for additional siblings.

BOY

How to sign it
Index finger sweeps under your chin from left to right.

GIRL

How to sign it
Index finger makes two small strokes down from your cheek towards your mouth.

Some grandparents will want to participate in every area of their grandchild's development, others can be sceptical at first about what they may see as 'a new fad of the modern age'. However, once a baby starts signing and begins to communicate, it is amazing how many sceptics change their minds!

GRANDAD/GRANDPA, ETC.

How to sign it
With fingers spread apart, hand sideways on, put the tip of your thumb on your forehead, and move your hand forwards and down making small arcs in front of you.

Figure 5.2 Grandad.

GRANDMA/NANNA, ETC.

How to sign it
With fingers spread, hand facing sideways, make small arc movements down from your chin.

> ## Top tip
> As the signs for Grandma and Grandad are similar, here is a top tip to help you remember which way round to sign them: Grandad is a thinker – so comes down from his head, Grandma is a talker – so the sign comes down from her chin!

Below are a few additional signs that you might find helpful for special people in your baby's life. Remember if you have a lot of close family you will need to be inventive with additional traits and characteristics. However, do keep to one sign per person. It is not necessary to sign 'Auntie' and then 'J' for Jo, for example, just choose one sign and say 'Auntie Jo'.

AUNTIE

How to sign it
With index and middle finger bent and slightly apart, tap your chin.

UNCLE

How to sign it
Index finger brushes back of other little finger twice.

COUSIN

How to sign it
Make a 'C' shape with your thumb and forefinger, and brush this twice under your chin.

FRIEND

How to sign it
Clasp one hand with the other – as if shaking hands – mime this up and down.

Figure 5.3 Friend.

Baby's own picture book

You may be surprised at how many babies appreciate having a personal 'special friends and family' picture book. It may even become their most treasured possession. Use a simple slip-in photo album, and either print off additional photos of friends and family, or use photos that you may have put aside for a variety of reasons – perhaps they were just not good enough for your 'official' family album.

Some families are quite complex in the number of grandparents they have, so using photos to differentiate between Granddad, Grandpa and Grandpops, for example, can be a great way to help your child use the right sign for each person. The album also has the advantage of giving you more opportunities to use the sign and word other than just when the person comes to visit. This will help to reinforce the signs and give your child extra practice in saying the words. And before too long your baby may be saying the names of friends and family and dropping the signs altogether – a delight for any grandparent who hears their name being spoken.

> **REMEMBER: Babies will sign and say words for things that interest them, so people are likely to feature highly on any baby's list.**

So try it for yourself. An album of your baby's own can become a precious resource and makes lovely bedtime reading with plenty of opportunity to talk about loved ones and reinforce the signs which you may like to choose from those shown at the beginning of this chapter.

Signing in a nursery setting

If your baby spends some time in the care of others who may not use signs with them, don't let that give you an excuse to be inconsistent yourself. You are still probably spending more than enough time with your baby to make baby signing worthwhile. Morning and evening routines, mealtimes and bathtimes all offer ideal opportunities to reinforce signs and can make your time together even more special. If whoever is looking after your child (nursery, childminder or grandparent) is happy to use a few signs too then that is a wonderful benefit. You can make it as easy as possible for them by printing out a page or two of your baby's favourite signs from the online dictionary on the website (www.singandsign.com), by showing them the Sing and Sign DVD or, indeed, by providing them with a copy of this book.

Many nurseries around the country understand the benefit, for staff and children, of adopting some simple signs as part of the day's regular routines. This helps the children anticipate what will happen next and understand boundaries, as well as helping to promote a calm atmosphere. Sing and Sign offers a Nursery Affiliation Programme and if your nursery would like to know more about how baby signing can help in childcare, they may contact your Sing and Sign teacher or visit the Sing and Sign website.

> We began signing with Isaac in Switzerland where he went to an all German-speaking crêche. We always spoke English at home. Once when I picked him up from the crêche he signed to me 'happy' and 'friends'. 'Friend' was our word for the crêche, so he was signing to me that he was happy at friends. This not only brought tears to my eyes (as one never really knows if one's baby is happy to go to crêche!), but it was the first time that he put two signs together!
>
> Louise Joyce

In recent years there has been so much more research on how children learn and the different learning styles that can be adopted. The main ways of learning that researchers have identified are: visual (seeing), auditory (hearing), kinaesthetic (moving) and tactile (touching).

Those who prefer a visual learning style:

- ▶ *look at the teacher's face intently*
- ▶ *like looking at wall displays, books, etc. and will recall information by remembering how it was set out on a page*
- ▶ *often recognize words by sight.*

Those who prefer an auditory learning style:

- ▶ *like the teacher to provide verbal instructions*
- ▶ *like dialogues, discussions and plays*
- ▶ *solve problems by talking about them*
- ▶ *use rhythm and sound as memory aids.*

Those who prefer a kinaesthetic learning style:

> ▸ *learn best when they are involved or active*
> ▸ *find it difficult to sit still for long periods*
> ▸ *use movement as a memory aid.*

Those who have a tactile learning style:

> ▸ *use writing and drawing as memory aids*
> ▸ *learn well in hands-on activities such as projects and demonstrations.*

By signing with your child, whether in a more formal nursery setting, or in the comfort of your own home, you are giving your child the opportunity to see, hear and do. Whenever he has a tough thing to learn – maybe he has trouble with his alphabet, difficulty remembering a song or there is a spelling he is stumbling over – signing can add an extra dimension to his learning. He hears what he is being told, but he also sees it and is involved if he signs it himself.

If you have a creative child who finds it a little difficult to 'tune in' to the logical brain processes often required in school learning, he will often excel at the more holistic approach that signing gives, thus also boosting his self-esteem. Using sign and speech together helps connections between logical and creative thought processes.

I first heard about baby signing when I was working in a nursery in Bristol. Signing was used with some of the children, and we all found signing really fun and helpful. After starting in a new nanny job, I started to use a few of the signs that I remembered. It was surprising how fast the baby picked them up.

Kathryn Furber

Bilingual babies

Young children absorb everything they hear, see and feel and they keep it forever. The unique (pure) sounds of language are acquired with ease when learning during childhood, so by beginning to learn a second language early, children gain heaps of confidence and are able to learn correct pronunciation of different languages which can be extremely difficult to master at a later stage.

For a child who is not just learning a second language but is being brought up in a bilingual family, signing can be invaluable. Many bilingual children begin to acquire speech a little later than children of the same age who are only being taught their mother tongue. Signing with a bilingual child helps the child to connect the two (or more) languages. The sign acts as an anchor for understanding the different languages. For example, if you point to a picture of a cow, and use the sign and say 'cow' in English and then use the same sign and say 'vaca', a toddler can easily understand that the sign stays the same whether you are speaking English or Spanish.

That very understanding will trigger the essential abstract thinking skills that are the basic tools for further learning.

I am Dutch and am bringing my kids up to be bilingual. This is one of the main reasons that I looked into baby signing, as I've always been told that bilingual kids tend to speak later because it takes that little bit longer to work the differences out, and I wanted a way to communicate with them while they were doing this. I started signing with my daughter when she was six to seven months old, and she started to sign back to me at 11 months ('milk' was her first sign). Once she started she quickly learned other signs, and at 14 months (I'll always remember this), we were going to read a story, and I opened the cover of the book we were going to read. She then signed rabbit, and I was wondering why, as there weren't really any pictures or anything to be seen yet, or so I thought, because round the edge of the page was this tiny border with pictures that are important to a baby's world, among them a rabbit. This really brought home to me what great observers children are and how, where we tend to only see the big picture, they see all the small details first. Needless to say, my daughter started talking at round about 18 months and has always been a great communicator
(Contd)

in both English and Dutch (this is not just a proud mummy speaking as everyone including the health visitor has commented on this). I then continued to sign with her brother when he was born, and even though he started to sign later (at 14 months) and never used as many signs as his big sister (he did know them all as he has used them on occasion), at two he is now a very clear speaker too, and hardly ever stops (sometimes I almost wonder if I shouldn't have done the signing!).

Being a bilingual family can be such fun – when either of my children would start telling me something, I wouldn't always know if they were talking English, Dutch or just baby babble. In those situations I found if I threw in a sign here and there, it could really clear things up.

Paula White

There is scientific evidence that children who are exposed to a second language from an early age not only achieve much better results in languages, but also in maths, science and music. It helps in general to build brainpower and cognitive skills. If you add signing into the equation, it enables clearer communication and clarity when you may not be sure what language your baby may be speaking.

Twins and multiple births

Multiple-birth parents are usually aware of the importance of helping each child develop their individuality while at the same time respecting the uniqueness of being a multiple. However, fostering individuality is easier said than done, and this also relates to acquiring language. You may have heard that multiple-birth children talk later than their single counterparts. Indeed, multiples acquire language just as single-born children do, though they often develop it at a slower pace. Even though multiples tend to make sounds and gestures early on to each other, they often say their first word (other than 'mama' or 'dada') about a month later than most single-born children. Language development, whether that be signing or speech, is a rewarding way to bring a closeness and intimacy with each other, as Helen describes with her twins in the following example.

Georgina had her favourite caterpillar glove puppet and was sitting close to Thomas who was playing with his dummy. Georgina turned around and Thomas reached forward and took her caterpillar. When Georgina looked back and saw it was gone she naturally looked at Thomas. Thomas smiled at her and signed 'gone' and 'where' and then laughed. He reached behind him and got the caterpillar and gave it a kiss (which Georgina likes to do). Thomas showed the caterpillar to Georgina and then hid it again and repeated the signs 'gone' and 'where' – they both laughed and Georgina signed 'more'. They played this game for about five minutes and it was so lovely to watch.

When Thomas and Georgina were about 14 months old we were at The Mall in Bristol (a big shopping complex) and the children were looking around at things. Thomas tapped Georgina on the arm – as they were sitting side by side – and signed 'crocodile' to her. Then he called me and signed 'crocodile'. I couldn't see a crocodile anywhere and asked them both again. Thomas signed 'crocodile' to Georgina again and she said 'des' ('yes') while looking at me and they both then pointed at a man who was wearing a Lacoste emblem on his T-shirt.

Helen Hill

It is often reported that twins and children of multiple births will create a 'language' of words and sentences that only they can understand. In actual fact this is generally the use of immature or incorrect speech patterns, vocabulary or grammar when learning to talk. This is primarily due to multiples not having as many chances as single-born children to interact directly and individually with their parents. They will inevitably spend more time listening and communicating to each other than single-born children. Over time and during interaction with each other, words become warped, and speech is not being corrected in the same way it might be if you had a single baby. This phenomenon is sometimes known as 'twin-talk'. Up to half of twins who use twin talk will also have a speech and language difficulty. However, it is important to note that this may also be due to other factors, such as the fact that many twins or multiple births are premature, which can provide its own challenges. For many parents of twins, speech and language difficulties won't be an issue at all, but being aware of statistics such as these is often half the battle to avoiding potential problems.

So, if you are a parent of twins, how can you enhance your children's communication? Try to use as many signs as possible within your daily routines, but also try to schedule in as much individual time with your babies as possible – maybe by taking just one child shopping, and using the opportunity to slow your speech and give more eye contact to the one child. Try to fit in as much one-to-one time as you can, singing and using a lot of eye contact at times such as nappy changing.

I wasn't expecting to gain anything from baby signing, it was just something to do on a Wednesday morning involving singing and music with my twin girls. However, using signing has helped Ella, Freya, myself and our family to communicate with each other effectively and has dramatically reduced frustration through lack of understanding. It has been so rewarding.

Signing helped us in a situation with the youngest of our twins. It was about five months into the classes and Ella had been admitted into hospital with an infection and high temperature. The medical staff and I were trying to find out the cause of the illness and as Ella was only 11 months old she was unable to communicate verbally what the problem was. Ella was getting increasingly irritable and I continued to try and pacify her. I asked her on numerous occasions 'where does it hurt' but to no avail.

Ella then caught my attention by using the sign for 'ouch/pain' near her stomach and then used the sign for 'drink' to indicate she was thirsty. She was given some water, drank it and then signed to me 'more', 'drink' and again did the 'ouch/pain' sign.

I signed back to Ella to get a clearer understanding of what she was trying to tell me and she confirmed by signing it ('pain') again. The doctors were intrigued and asked what I was doing and I explained that we had been attending signing classes in Bristol and 'translated' what Ella was signing and requested that they check that specific area on her stomach. We subsequently found out that Ella had developed a urinary tract infection which needed specific treatment!

Without baby signing it may have taken some time to find out what the problem was and caused Ella a lot more upset.

Ella and Freya have grown and developed in their confidence and social interaction, and their speech has increased along with their enthusiasm for all things musical. I put this all down to the fun time we have all had with Sing and Sign – we shall all really miss the classes when we leave.

Nayna Patel with Ella and Freya

Signing dads

The modern dad is generally considered to be different from those a generation ago. Dads today are often perceived to have a more active role in their child's life. With so many parents going to work, however, many now do not have the luxury of attending mid-week groups, and this would be especially true for fathers.

The aim of this book is to bridge the gap for those parents who are unable to attend such mid-week groups, and enable dads (or other secondary carers) to learn the signs, thus providing continuity for the child. In this way all key people can be involved in actively communicating with the child, before he is able to verbally express himself.

Not being a dad myself, I asked a couple of dads, both in different situations, to tell you a little bit of their own experience of baby signing. I have left this very much in their own words in order for them to convey to you what they feel is important.

Naturally as a parent you want the best for your child, you want to understand their needs and give them the best possible start. For me this was quite difficult as I was often at work during the day while my wife was the main carer at home.

That said, when my boys were babies, signing became an essential form of communication and allowed us to understand their needs and them to understand us. The crying was often eventually accompanied by a sign, so you then knew the reason for the screams and weren't merely grasping the air in frustration for answers.

My first experience of signing was coming in from work and seeing my boys sitting in front of a video called 'Sing and Sign' and my wife sitting with them talking and using exaggerated body language and signs which they seemed to be attentive to. On the video there were songs being accompanied by signing and my eldest son was transfixed to what was being communicated. Suddenly a whole new world was being unravelled before me and I began to communicate with my son through signs I was learning from the video and more importantly those my wife was teaching me.

From something as simple as asking for food or milk to expressing a desire for 'more', it was amazing the amount of visual language my children picked up. Quite often signing became second nature, particularly with Joseph who was later diagnosed with hearing loss.

There were certain times in the evening, after work, that I spent with the boys alone. For instance, at bathtime I found I could introduce signs I had been taught for certain toys like boats and signs for washing. At bedtime both my wife and I would read stories which were quite vocal, so more often than not the signing was accompanied by loud noises to complement the bedtime story.

The older my children became the more signs became second nature. It alleviated many temper tantrums as my sons could sign when asked what it was that was upsetting them. It is equally important for the parent who is not the primary carer to keep up the signing and give the child a level of consistency. In using signing it was important that my wife showed me the signs she had learnt so that we were acting in the same way.

Lack of time is not an excuse for either parent: it will help you bond with your child and help to keep continuity in the family unit. I cannot advocate enough the benefits of signing which make the effort and time put in worthwhile.

Mick Melville-Reed, dad to Jacob, Joseph, Talitha and Jediah

The term 'parenthood' is a problematic one to define because we all have differing experiences depending on who we are: whether we are mum or dad, whether we are the 'primary carer', or perhaps we work all week and only 'see the kids at the weekend'.

How does a dad's experience as a parent differ from that of a mum's?

Who is the primary carer/secondary carer?

Who is at home? Who works elsewhere all day?

Some working/commuting dads only see kids at breakfast/bedtime/weekends...

If you are a dad, working all week, signing can be a good way for you to 'catch up' by being involved in an established link between mum and baby.

Why is it important for dads to sign with their child? – Signing can quickly become a common household language (not to sign would mean 'exclusion'), as well as giving 'continuity' between parents for the child.

(Contd)

Tabitha's vocabulary and sign repertoire was very large very early on – all children sign/walk/talk at different rates, but we felt Tabitha was definitely advantaged by word/sign stimulation from an early stage.

One major benefit of signing is that it alleviates frustration at not being understood and initially helps parents to 'underline' the meaning of a sentence with a simple sign; eventually the child learns to sign back and begins to discover the rewards of cross communication (i.e. getting what they are trying to ask for).

Later on, signing helps to communicate difficult sounding words when learning phonics and speech sounds – gives the child the confidence to attempt to pronounce the word because they have the sign to back up their intended meaning.

As Tabitha grew, signs fell away with progression of her speech – but with arrival of 'number two' (Tilly), Tabitha 'remembered' her old signing ways to communicate with her new sister.

Tilly was a typical 'second child' – she signed, walked and talked later because she liked to watch her older sibling do it all for her.

Christian Cotton, dad to Tabitha and Tilly

Both Mick and Christian have found signing with their children beneficial, and are pleased they took the time and effort to learn some simple signs. Time can play a large factor when choosing to sign with your baby. Many fathers have an hour snatched before work, a few hours snatched after work and before bed, and then the so important weekends that form the primary time to be with their children.

Insight
It cannot be overstated how spending small amounts of time learning signs and developing your repertoire will reap huge rewards when interacting with your baby.

Take a few moments to think about the time that you spend with your baby. What is it that you spend your time doing? Feeding? Playing? Bathing? Do you use the time to go out, or read to your child? Is there a particular routine that you follow? Maybe your special time with your baby is their night-time routine? Whatever it is, you should be able to find some signs in this book that you can incorporate into your individual time with your baby. Start with maybe two or three signs, and then add to them as you become more confident. You may be surprised at the positive difference this can make with your child, and the improvements it can make to your bond.

TEST YOUR KNOWLEDGE

1 *How can you enrich your baby's excitement and anticipation at seeing favourite friends and relatives?*

2 *The signs for Grandma and Grandad are similar, what is an easy way to remember the difference?*

3 *How can you create signs for significant people in your baby's life?*

4 *What benefit is there in giving your child a photo album of special people in their life?*

5 *How does using signs with pre-verbal babies benefit children in a nursery setting?*

6 *If your child is regularly being looked after by someone who is unfamiliar with signing, in what practical ways can you help to introduce them to signing with your child?*

7 *What impact do the different learning styles have on signing with your baby and perhaps older child?*

8 *What benefit can signing have in a bilingual family?*

9 *What are some of the unique challenges facing parents of twins with regard to speech and language?*

10 *Why is it important for dads to learn how to sign and how can they best achieve this?*

See answer section at the back of the book.

6

Special needs

In this chapter you will learn:
- *more about a few of the most common disabilities and disorders that affect children*
- *how signing has helped individual parents in specific situations*
- *how to identify a particular difficulty and what to do about it.*

This is a complex area to deal with, given the wide spectrum of disabilities and disorders, but it is an area that I certainly did not want to ignore. Signing programmes are regularly contacted by parents with babies and children who have Global Developmental Delay, Down Syndrome and hearing problems, to name but a few. Quite often these children have already been diagnosed, and parents are enquiring as to whether signing will benefit their child. It is important to say at this point that if you are at all concerned with your child's development or speech advancement, then it is always advisable to seek the advice of a health professional.

Obviously all children, whether they have specialized needs or not, will naturally develop at different rates, and this rate will, of course, be further impacted upon by any other health issues there may be. You may well be reading this chapter as a parent of a child with special needs, wondering if signing will help your particular situation. Naturally it would be impossible to give an outright yes or no, but from experience (and you can read other parents' own experiences in this chapter), the overwhelming majority of parents will say yes!

This section explains and introduces a few of the most common needs that lead parents to enquire about baby signing, and includes the voices of 'experts' in the field – mothers and fathers who have had to deal with these issues with their children. If you are a parent of a child with special needs, I hope you find something here to help and inspire you.

Maia was born with Treacher Collins Syndrome. Her ears are malformed yet she is able to hear well with her bone conductor hearing aid. She also has a tracheostomy to help her breathe and while this is in place she is unable to use her voice. Our motivation to use signing with Maia is twofold: we want to maximize her communication skills in light of both her hearing impairment and her temporary inability to speak; we imagine that signing will also support Maia's developing speech once the tracheostomy has been removed and we shall introduce Makaton signs (see Chapter 8) as she gets older.

We are certain that we would have begun using baby signing with a 'regular' baby as the benefits seem so great. With Maia, of course, it has been an important aspect of her upbringing from the earliest days and after months of singing and signing as often as we could it is very exciting to embark on our first conversations. She is now 14 months old and has upward of 15 signs – which she is very proud of! Some signs are still rather approximate but she frequently uses them in the correct context. Interestingly, she is most consistent when prompted by the accompanying song and she often babbles with her hands as if in practice.

We have no doubt that signing will ease Maia's frustration, develop her memory, help her confidence and increase her sensitivity towards non-verbal communication. Most importantly, for the time being, it is providing us with a great deal of fun and quality time together. We love the classes, and the warmth and understanding we have received from our

teacher and classmates have helped us through this challenging
year. It fills our hearts to see Maia making such enormous
progress after her traumatic start to life. It is also of great
comfort that baby signing is so popular and valued in the wider
community. It has made the experience of having a hearing/
voice-impaired child less isolating for us as we know that many
parents and children are avid signers as well.

Josie and Martin Tollner with Maia aged 14 months

Developmental Delay

Parents often have concerns about their children's development,
especially in a society where we seem to be constantly comparing
our children, checking to see which children of the same age
have attained a particular developmental milestone. This can cause
a great deal of anxiety in parents, especially if your child still hasn't
met the same milestone, possibly causing you to think that your
child is a little 'slow' for their age or 'seems behind'. It is important
to keep in mind that for each developmental milestone, there is
a range of ages at which a child will normally meet it. For example,
some children may walk as early as nine months, while others may
not walk until they are nearing 20 months old. Similarly, while
there are those who seem to have nailed speech at around
18 months and those who are still using very basic speech
at a much later age, both can still be classed to be within
'normal' range.

Insight

Some parents are acutely aware of their child's delay, while
other parents, particularly first-time parents who don't have
another sibling to compare with, may not be so aware of the
milestones. Books giving general guidelines on development
can be helpful, but remember they are only a guide and
children develop in different areas at different times. If you
are unsure about your baby's development then do seek
medical assurance.

Developmental Delay is usually a diagnosis made by a doctor based on strict guidelines. Usually when a child does not achieve one or more of their developmental milestones at the expected time, and it generally becomes an ongoing major delay in the process of their development, this is then called Developmental Delay. As developmental milestones are determined by the average age at which children attain each skill, not every child will reach them at the expected time. Statistically very few children will go on to be diagnosed with Developmental Delay or Global Developmental Delay. If your child is slightly or only temporarily lagging behind, that does not fall into the same category as Developmental Delay. Many children who fall into the second category will eventually develop normally over time, although maybe a little later than expected.

WHAT CAUSES DEVELOPMENTAL DELAY?

Developmental Delay can have many different causes, such as genetic (for example, Down Syndrome), or complications of pregnancy and birth (for example, prematurity or infections). Often, however, the specific cause is unknown. Some causes can be easily reversed if caught early enough, such as hearing loss from chronic ear infection.

Delay can occur in one or many areas – for example, motor, language, social or thinking skills. By definition, Global Developmental Delay implies that the child has delays in all areas of development.

Although a doctor diagnoses the condition, it is usually you, the parent, who is the first to notice that your child may not be progressing at the same rate as other children of the same age. It is vital that you talk with your doctor or health visitor about it. In some cases, this will be picked up at the regular developmental checks that babies have. It will probably take several visits and possibly a referral to a developmental paediatric specialist to be sure that the delay is not just a temporary lag. Special testing can also help gauge your child's developmental level in relation to the developmental milestones.

BENEFITS OF EARLY DIAGNOSIS

Early developmental intervention and instruction helps to influence a young, impressionable and receptive brain. It helps to maximize a child's developmental potential, and functional abilities, such as social communication, mobility and adaptive skills. It can be really important for parents to learn what 'normal' development is, and how their child is developing in relation to that. They are then in a much better position to be able to tailor their expectations to what their particular child can achieve, and provide stimulation and toys to match the child's own individual developmental milestones.

We are now very aware that the first three to five years of a child's life are an amazing time of development, and that what happens during those years stays with a child for a lifetime. That's why it is so important to watch for signs of delays in development, and to get help from professionals if you suspect problems. The sooner developmentally delayed children receive intervention, the better their progress will be.

While I was pregnant with Adam I had read about signing with babies and was very interested in it. It wasn't something I'd done with my other three children and so I thought I would give it a go!

I have been attending signing classes since Adam was seven months old – he is now nearly two and a half. At first I found it quite daunting trying to keep up and learn all these signs, but after a couple of weeks or so some started to sink in and the songs make them so much easier to learn! Adam was quite happy at this age to lie there and watch.

As a few months passed, Adam's development was noticeably delayed. All the other babies were beginning to sign and as we progressed to the Improvers class some of them were saying words too – Adam was doing nothing. So we kept on going to the classes. We did three lots of Beginners and currently we are on our second Improvers! Earlier this year Adam finally did his first sign, which was 'duck', and has gone on to do a few more.

(Contd)

As we can see from Lisa's story, a developmental delay also impacted on the length of time it took for her son to learn to sign. Nevertheless, signing can become a vital part of the learning process and enable communication when speech may still be much further away.

Down Syndrome

It is often said that babies with Down Syndrome find it much harder to learn auditorily than they do visually, and with a large percentage of children with Down Syndrome having hearing problems, it therefore makes perfect sense to introduce signing alongside speech. Many children with Down Syndrome may have delayed speech with poor pronunciation, but depending on the severity of the condition, many will go on to intelligible speech. However, due to the low muscle tone of the face, smaller than average mouth cavity, and the shape and size of the tongue, speech does not generally come easily and quickly. Signing can be essential when trying to discriminate between similar-sounding words and sounds.

A few months after starting signing, Neve regularly used about 12 signs. We took her to visit my cousin who has Down Syndrome. They had disappeared behind a chair and were obviously playing together, when I noticed they were actually

signing to one another. My cousin, Stella, uses Makaton
(see Chapter 8) to supplement her communication, and some
of the Sing and Sign signs were recognizable to her.

Vanessa Kreimeia

My son, Scott, was born with Down Syndrome and we were told
to sign to him from six months as we didn't know how much his
speech would be delayed. We began to learn Signalong when we
moved back to Edinburgh and it was only after I had my second
son, Tom, that I found Sing and Sign. Scott is now aged five and
at mainstream school. He still signs a lot and will sign 'cake' as
we arrive at a party, 'horse' as we are getting ready for riding,
and 'work' for daddy when he is at work, or 'plane' when he
is down in London. Scott's speech is still delayed and he still
gets speech and language therapy. He is beginning to use and
understand pronouns, developing short sentences, understands
taking turns and uses social words like sorry, excuse me, please
and thank you.

He has done so well recognizing and saying the seven Jolly
Phonics sets but still has difficulty with C, K and G.

He still signs a lot, using a boardmarker for a picture timetable
at home and school, and using symbols and gestures. He can
recognize his name, mummy, daddy, his brother Tom, numbers
one to five and he can almost write his own name. His school
and ASN (additional support needs) teacher all say he is
surpassing his IEP (individual education plan) targets.

He has inspired us all to sign to each other when we are out of
hearing distance. For example, when I am trying to get Graham
or the boys' attention to come in for dinner, drink, tea, etc. or
when they are inside and I am out, or at the other end of the
garden (we have 3 acres!), we sign to convey what we want to
say. Signing is now part of our lives and we don't know what we
would do without it!

Caroline Forbes with Scott and Ben

Vanessa and Caroline mention sign supporting systems – namely Signalong and Makaton. Both these systems are compatible with the signs shown in *Sign with Your Baby* and Sing and Sign. These systems are designed for use with speech, and therefore the keyword approach to signing that is used throughout this book is entirely appropriate. Children with Down Syndrome may be advised to learn Makaton or another sign support system. A few signs may vary, and this is largely due to the dexterity of a small baby's hand. For further information on signing systems, refer to Chapter 8 where this subject is covered in more detail.

Please note: Down Syndrome (which is the correct terminology) is commonly referred to as Down's Syndrome in British English.

Speech delay

It is known that approximately 5 to 10 per cent of children have a developmental disability that causes a delay in their speech and language development. As with other areas, it is often the parents who are the first to notice that their child is not developing language skills at the same rate as similarly aged children and will describe their child as 'not talking', 'a late talker', or 'not speaking yet'. However, as we have already discovered in previous chapters, it is important to bear in mind that a child's language development involves more than just speech. It also includes other forms of communication, such as sign language, visual/pointing skills, and then as they get older, other skills such as writing.

WHAT CAUSES SPEECH DELAY?

It is recognized that there are three main areas that can cause speech delay in children. These are problems with the:

▸ **output** *of speech (anatomical problems with the vocal cords, etc.)*
▸ **input** *of speech (such as hearing loss)*
▸ **processing** *of speech (cognitive delay and developmental language disorders).*

Alongside this, there are two main types of speech delay:

1 **Expressive delay** – *the inability to generate speech.*
2 **Receptive delay** – *the inability to decode or understand the speech of others.*

Of course, some children may have a delay with a mix of both types, which is known as mixed expressive/receptive delay.

Most children with speech delays have developmental language disorders (DLD), with an inability to generate speech. This is known as expressive delay. The good news is that children with expressive delay will generally meet normal age-appropriate visual-language skills, which could be recognizing parents and objects, responding to others' facial expressions, as well as following instructions that are accompanied with a gesture or sign indicating what you want done. These children will seem to have normal comprehension or understanding of other people's speech, and will generally be meeting all other normal age-appropriate auditory receptive skills (recognizing and turning toward sounds, following one- or two-step commands without a gesture, pointing to named body parts and objects). With early intervention of specialists and a good speech therapist, most of these children will have improved speech by the time they begin school and their speech will ultimately become normal.

Some children with an expressive delay are just 'late talkers' and have a delay in their speech development. These children will develop normal speech and language skills as they get older without any treatment. Unfortunately, there is no way to differentiate children with this type of delay, whose speech will improve without intervention, from those children who will require treatment. You can only tell in hindsight and it is not advisable just to 'wait and see' whether your child's speech will improve.

Another important cause of speech delay is hearing problems, and so all children suspected of having a speech or language delay should have their hearing formally tested. This can be arranged through your GP or health visitor. It is not enough that you think your child hears because she responds to you when you call her from another room, or responds when she hears a dog bark, or you clap your hands.

> **Insight**
>
> My own son's hearing seemed to vary depending on the day, weather or type of sound. I had convinced myself he could hear fine (or it was just childhood selective hearing!). In fact he had a significant hearing loss due to glue ear, so his hearing did in fact fluctuate according to how much fluid was in his ear. It is important to let the experts check it out if you have any concerns.

There are other causes of speech delays, but things that don't cause speech delays are a child being 'tongue-tied', being 'lazy', having a lot of siblings that 'talk for her', or living in a bilingual family.

> **Insight**
>
> A common misconception is that if your child is already having problems talking, then signing will only inhibit them further. Maybe it is helpful to consider it in another way: if you child is already having problems with speech, then how wonderful to provide them with the opportunity to be able to communicate.
>
> The frustration that a child with verbal language difficulties experiences can be huge – providing them with a way to effectively communicate can provide enormous relief.

Premature babies

A premature baby, or 'premie' as they are often affectionately called, is born before the 37th week of pregnancy. Premature birth occurs in between 8 and 10 per cent of all pregnancies in the UK. Because they are born too early, premies weigh much less than full-term babies. Premature infants are therefore prone to a number of health problems, mostly because their internal organs aren't completely ready to function on their own. The more mature your baby is at birth, the more likely it is that she will not have any medical problems.

When monitoring premature babies, careful attention is paid to the development of the nervous system, including the achievement of motor skills such as smiling, sitting and walking, as well as the positioning and tone of the muscles.

Speech and behavioural development are also important areas during follow-up. Some premature infants may require speech therapy or physical therapy as they grow up. Signing can prove a valuable part in aiding their development, as Katy found out in the following example.

As a mum of an eight-week premature baby, I was worried about his development and despite knowing that his development at age six months was likely to be that of a four-month-old, I didn't want it to be, because he had still been here for six months. I'm a great believer in baby signing, and took him to signing classes as I wanted to do anything I could to increase his chances of speaking early (well, when other babies his age did). It turned out that he said his first words, 'all gone', at age 13 months in the middle of a class when we put Jessie Cat back in the box. Interestingly, 'all gone' was also his first sign at age 11 months after finishing his dinner. Now, at age 19 months, he can say anything he wants to, although the words he says regularly are words that we sign at classes and home.

Katy Duckett

Insight

Katy made an interesting point in her story that I have heard echoed many times. Babies' first words are often those that they began signing. Generally as speech increases, signs will naturally decrease.

Deafness

Deafness comes in varying degrees, which are often described as mild, moderate, severe and profound. Hearing levels are often described in terms of decibels. During this section I have used the word 'deaf' to cover all types and degrees of hearing loss.

There are generally two types of deafness:

1   *Sensori-neural deafness, or nerve deafness as it is sometimes called, is a hearing loss in the inner ear. This usually means that the cochlea in the inner ear is not working properly.*
2   *Conductive deafness means that sound cannot pass through the outer and middle ear into the inner ear. This is often caused by blockages such as wax in the outer ear, or fluid in the middle ear (glue ear – see page 148).*

There are over 35,000 deaf children in the UK, with at least two deaf children being born each day. Of these children, 90 per cent are born to hearing parents with little experience of deafness. Very few deaf children have no useful hearing. Most deaf children can hear some sounds at certain frequencies and volumes, and with the use of hearing aids they are often able to hear more sounds.

My son was born ten weeks early and, possibly due to him having to be resuscitated at birth, was born with a moderate/severe hearing loss. We didn't find out until he was two, so we were so fortunate that we had decided to Sing and Sign with our baby before we knew we would come to rely on it as the only form of communication for quite a while! All of Joseph's was delayed, not just speech and language, and it took a few months to get his first sign – 'more' food! After that the signs flowed and then the speech arrived! Joseph is almost five now and as his speech is often unclear he will still sign to get his point across.

As Joseph is being brought up as a 'deaf child with speech' he didn't need to learn sign language, but knowing basic signs has helped him communicate with deaf children who sign, who we inevitably meet at deaf clubs, etc. We were very aware that Sing and Sign used signs that were based on Makaton, but Makaton is based on BSL (British Sign Language) and most of the animals and suchlike are the same!

I cannot thank Sing and Sign enough for making signing fun and easy to learn, and helping us through all those frustrating times that could have been so much worse without the communication that we had worked on!

I just wish I had signed with my first child who had no speech and language delays. I am positive it would have lessened those terrible twos tantrums!

Vicki Melville-Reed, mum to Jacob, Joseph, Talitha and Jediah

Deafness makes it harder for children to learn to communicate and many families face challenges in establishing communication with their deaf child. You will find some helpful tips at the end of this chapter on how to aid communication with a deaf child. Deaf children need to have access to fluent language so that they can develop good communication and language skills. This could either be through spoken language, sign language or both together.

Insight

As Sing and Sign starts with babies as young as six months, many parents with deaf children have found it an invaluable resource, aiding communication with their child. Some will go on to learn the formal language for deaf people, BSL (British Sign Language), while others will use signing support systems (a further explanation of which can be found in Chapter 8).

There is a huge amount of support available for deaf children. Your GP, health visitor or local hospital should be able to point you in the right direction, and the National Deaf Children's Society is an invaluable resource for parents too (www.ndcs.org.uk).

My brother, Richard, is 17 months younger than me and is profoundly deaf. In the 1970s the 'experts' recommended that my parents use an oral/aural approach as 'signing would discourage speech'. As kids we communicated easily through lip-reading and our own gestural system, despite being told back then to 'sit on your hands'. Once at school, Richard quickly started to pick up signs from other children and he would share these with me. He continued in the oral system but it became more and more clear to us that the children from deaf families where signing was their first language were the most sociable and rounded human beings: they were always involved in family discussions (where we had to remember to include Richard, as he would miss so much when we were just talking); they absorbed general knowledge from observing the conversations around them, just as hearing children overhear facts and opinions; and they had a stronger sense of identity from being included, rather than always being on the periphery. My experience with my brother led me to decide to become a Teacher of the Deaf, but in the 1980s this qualification didn't actually include sign language training! In 1992 I took my British Sign Language Stage 1 exam (and later my Stage 2) and went to work in a Total Communication school for deaf children. My brother now works in computer-aided design in an office full of hearing people with whom he communicates by email and lip-reading! But his social life is mostly within the deaf world where he is most comfortable with his own language, BSL.

Julie Warriner

Glue ear

Glue ear is a very common condition, with one in five children (especially pre-school children) suffering from it. This is also by far the most common cause of mild hearing loss in babies and children. Glue ear is essentially a build-up of sticky fluid behind the eardrum. The space behind the ear drum (middle ear) is normally full of air, allowing the drum to vibrate. Air gets into the middle ear through a tube which leads to the back of the nose, close to the adenoids. The tube opens when you swallow, yawn or blow your nose but it often doesn't work very well in children meaning that air cannot get into the middle ear, which fills up with fluid instead. This fluid 'glue' of glue ear is what causes mild to moderate hearing difficulty.

I decided to sign with Thomas because of my background as a Teacher of the Deaf and my knowledge of signing. Someone told me about the Sing and Sign video and that got me started! I had no idea at the time that Thomas would turn out to have hearing difficulties (glue ear) but I'm sure all the extra input from the signing has counteracted any possible language difficulties that may have arisen from the condition. As a baby Thomas had constant ear infections and burst eardrums. At three he is now being considered for grommets. He has also had a speech and language therapy assessment due to some difficulties with active nasal fricatives (v, b, f, s), which is all connected to his constant colds and breathing difficulties. The speech therapist confirmed what I know: that despite a few pronunciation problems and the fluctuating hearing, he has incredible language and vocabulary for a child who is not yet four! I wholeheartedly believe that baby signing has given him the best possible start.

Julie Warriner

The most common cause of glue ear in children is congestion of the nose, causing blockage of the tubes, frequent colds or flu (which is why glue ear is particularly common in winter) or allergies, hay fever, sinusitis or recurrent ear infections. Smoking in the household is also known to be a contributing factor.

The good news is that glue ear can clear up of its own accord, usually after a few weeks, although it can be months or sometimes years, but most will need no treatment. It is unusual after the age of eight and seldom has any harmful long-term effect on the ears. It is only when the hearing loss is persistent and adversely affecting the child's speech, behaviour or education that treatment may be necessary – usually in the form of grommets.

As a family we were thrust into the realms of having a child with a significant hearing loss. As Josiah was our second child we were already in the habit of signing and so continued signing with him until his speech was well developed. He started signing very early, but maintained only a handful of signs until he was almost 14 months when he really took off – so different from our experiences with our first son who signed proficiently from seven months! He seemed to speak quite early and had a very good comprehension of language.

At around two and a half years of age, things were progressing well for Josiah, and then he had an ear infection – his first and last. It did seem to affect his hearing, but that was only to be expected. It was a few months down the line when we started to notice that he still hadn't got his hearing back to normal, but by then we were more concerned about other areas of his behaviour. He had always been a very happy, contented child, growing into a lovely toddler and responding well to people. His behaviour seemed to deteriorate rapidly. He was prone to awful temper tantrums and unexplained episodes of crying – he also went from being almost totally toilet-trained to having to go back into nappies – it seemed like within a few short months, someone had transported my little boy.

During this time my best friend (who, incidentally, has a deaf child with moderate to severe hearing loss) questioned me over my son's hearing. To my shame I kept ignoring this, telling her he was fine. In reality there were times when he did seem to hear quite well and other times when he seemed to ignore you completely. My reasoning was that all children have 'selective deafness', especially when it is something they don't want to hear!

It was only when our health visitor contacted us to find out how things were going, that I mentioned he was still in nappies, that his behaviour was absolutely terrible, and that I wasn't sure he was hearing everything we were saying, although I still wasn't fully convinced as this seemed to fluctuate. He also had periods when he was crying at night and was getting more difficult to settle. I felt instead of growing and developing, in a short time my little boy was regressing, and by now his speech was affected. Certain words he used to pronounce clearly, we were now struggling with. We had naturally gone back to using signing a little more with him.

After a few questions the health visitor said she would like to refer him for a hearing test at the hospital. Surely if he had a hearing loss then it would be consistent? I have to say at this time, a good six months from his initial, and only, ear infection, I was beginning to struggle in my relationship with him. Everything I tried didn't really seem to work. He became more distant, sometimes in his own little world where you would feel like you were intruding. He was also becoming increasingly clumsy, falling over things – however, on the whole, we struggled on, until the day of his hearing test.

Even at this point, I thought the hospital tests might find he had a mild hearing loss in one ear, but certainly not both. During the test he seemed unable to follow simple commands the audiologist asked of him. He explained that he thought he was just a little young for some of these tests. I assured him he was more than capable of those instructions. I therefore made Jos look at me (so natural with signing!) and using words and signs, told him what he needed to do – he did it perfectly! I told the audiologist that he obviously couldn't hear his commands, but he was incredibly capable. When it came to measuring the amount of air passing through the middle ear we were shocked to discover there wasn't any air passing through in either ear. In fact, Jos was hearing at a very low level, being classed as moderately verging on severely deaf. I was so shocked! The consultation seemed to finish quite quickly and we were given several leaflets on glue ear. Following advice we asked about the 'speech banana', an easy reference guide to show what sort of sounds, consonants and vowels a child is hearing. Jos was only hearing about five letters.

Following this consultation I went through a range of emotions. Partly guilt from not pursing things further, and amazement that

(Contd)

I had informed other parents on these types of issues, urging them to seek professional advice, but been blind to it in my own son. I also felt incredibly protective of him, and relieved it was nothing too serious. I then, of course, wanted to do all I could for him in the intervening process. Although the initial diagnosis with regard to his hearing loss wasn't good, the overall outcome is normally excellent, with most children not having further problems after treatment.

We also went on to talk to his playgroup about how they could help him using more signs which we printed from the Sing and Sign website (www.singandsign.com) and making sure he was looking at them when they were giving instructions (see 'Aiding communication with a deaf child' at the end of this chapter). We also received a referral for speech therapy. In addition to this, we went back to using many more signs with Jos. However, he was now three years old, and I had to learn new signs over and above the signs we had previously learnt with him as a young baby, as I now required additional signs that were developmentally appropriate for him.

Almost a year from his first infection he was booked in to have grommets fitted. This is quite a simple procedure and takes about half an hour, although it's never easy as a parent watching your child being anaesthetised and going into theatre. Signing again was invaluable. Jos very clearly demonstrated to the nurses that he was not going to go on to the bed – any suggestion, and he clearly said and signed 'NO'!

The good news, as happens with many children who have glue ear, is that things immediately went back to normal, and I had my lovely little boy back again. Seven months on, however, we have noticed he again is not hearing words correctly, waking more at night, so we are off to visit the consultant again – we might need the next size up in grommets.

SYMPTOMS OF GLUE EAR

▸ *Fluctuating hearing loss.*
▸ *Brief episodes of earache, lasting two to three hours,*
  often at night.

- *Inability to listen or pay attention. Tendency to daydream.*
- *Behaviour problems/tantrums.*
- *Recurrent ear infections.*
- *Speech problems, especially in young children, usually mild. Difficulty in saying some of the quiet consonant sounds and in developing use of language generally.*
- *Poor balance.*

AIDING COMMUNICATION WITH A DEAF CHILD OR A CHILD WITH HEARING LOSS

Below are some points to remember when you are communicating with your child, or points to pass onto other caregivers. They are important because they give your child the best chance of understanding you. These apply to children who use either oral skills, such as speech and lip-reading, or use sign language, or to those children who use a combination of both.

- *Make sure that you have your child's attention before starting to sign or speak to her.*
- *Maintain good eye contact and speak clearly and naturally, keeping your voice up, but without shouting. Ensure only one person is speaking at a time.*
- *Tell everyone involved with your child, such as friends and family, playgroup, etc., about your child's condition, maybe using these helpful tips as a guide.*
- *If your child does not understand a word or sign, try to use a different one with the same meaning.*
- *Try to keep background noise to a minimum. Turn off the TV when talking. Sounds bounce off hard surfaces, which can make listening difficult for children with hearing aids or for those with mild deafness who don't use hearing aids or amplification devices.*
- *Although communication may have been difficult, do remember to talk a lot to your child about what you are doing, or what your child is looking at or doing.*
- *Try to use signs and gestures with appropriate facial expressions to support what you are saying – remember deaf children rely so much more on visual clues.*

- ▶ *Make sure your child knows when there is a new topic of conversation so that she understands the context.*
- ▶ *Be patient. Try not to get angry when your child keeps saying 'What?', 'Pardon' or 'Uhhh'.*
- ▶ *Take extra care when out and about with your child, especially around traffic – she may not be able to hear you clearly in a busy street.*

TEST YOUR KNOWLEDGE

1 *If you are unsure about your child's rate of development and advancement, what is the best course of action?*

2 *Give a brief description of Developmental Delay.*

3 *What is the difference between Developmental Delay and Global Developmental Delay?*

4 *What impact can a diagnosis of Development Delay have on a child's ability to sign?*

5 *What are the most formative years of a child's development, and why is this age so important?*

6 *Name two sign supporting systems that are compatible with signs shown in this book.*

7 *A common misconception is that if your child is already having problems talking, then signing will only inhibit them further. How could you answer these misconceptions?*

8 *What is the most common cause for mild to moderate hearing loss in babies and young children?*

9 *Give three symptoms of this condition.*

10 *Name three ways to aid communication with a child who has hearing loss.*

See answer section at the back of the book.

7

Signing with older children

In this chapter you will learn:
- *how to use signs with emerging speech*
- *the benefits of signing and reading*
- *developmentally appropriate signs.*

Getting ready for speech

Learning to talk is a long journey for children – they will understand more than they are able to say, and those early words can be difficult for you to understand. You may not know if your child is saying 'buh' for ball, Barney, the preferred toy of the day, or even their favourite book. Signing can be fantastic in distinguishing what your child's ambiguous sounding word actually means, and therefore enabling you to accurately decipher what it is they want. It also provides an important opportunity for you to correctly reinforce the spoken word. This obviously lessens frustration on both sides enormously and will therefore help to increase your bond. Parents of signing children will often testify that their children don't have temper tantrums as a result not being understood, they just have them as a result of being told 'no' or not getting their own way!

Most children follow typical patterns of speech sound development, called phonological processes, which are a normal part of the speech development process. Some patterns can include sound or syllable substitutions, omissions or additions.

As we have discovered, a baby's first word tends to appear around his first birthday, with a more rapid growth of vocabulary at around 18 months. So children will often learn 'true words' mixed with jargon or 'babbling' to try and imitate the adult conversations they hear around them. For example, 'ahhh oooo' is unrecognizable as 'thank you'. However, your baby will pick up on the vowels and probably mimic the intonation and lilt in your voice, therefore distinguishing it from true 'baby babble', and allowing it to be acknowledged as an attempt at 'thank you'. These early practice attempts at dialogue gradually develop into more intelligible speech.

Continually reinforcing signs with the spoken word encourages children to start vocalizing the words they have been signing, until they drop the signs altogether in favour of speech. Speech naturally takes over as the main form of communication, so you shouldn't be worried that if your child begins signing he will never stop, or will continue and use it in place of speech. If you are following guideline No. 3, 'Always say the word as you sign', your child will begin to pronounce words and use his hands less.

> At his 18-month check-up my son's speech and language development was very advanced for his years. We continued signing to him when he was learning his colours and phonics, even though his speech was very good, but obviously as soon as he could say certain words, the signs just naturally fell away.
>
> Catherine with her son Michael

Insight

We had the same result with my children at their 18-month checks, as have many other signing mums I have spoken with. It is regularly reported that babies who sign have language development and comprehension far beyond their natural age. This also confirms the results of the studies we looked at in Chapter 1.

How signing facilitates speech development

Compared to 30 years ago, there is now far more evidence that signing can and does aid the development and facilitation of speech, dispelling an earlier myth that signing might actually inhibit speech. Signs act as a go-between while learning spoken words, when both are consistently paired in teaching. In addition, the neurologically based links between manual activity and speech suggest that there is a natural affinity between the two modes of communication. A study by Reid (1984) found that not only were signs learnt more quickly than words, but that children who learnt signs first, subsequently found it easier to learn words. They seemed to have developed an understanding of the principle of labelling in sign, which is then transferred to the spoken word. Two other studies suggest that signing can directly facilitate articulatory skills, and that this effect may be due to the controlled movements of signing, providing a 'motor plan' for accompanying speech.

> **Insight**
>
> Many families have testified that their baby's first spoken words were those that were signed first too. It is almost as if by learning how to sign, the child has understood the pattern of early basic language skills. By putting many of the building blocks in place when signing, these children are further ahead than their peers when speech comes along.

Very soon toddlers and older children move from signing their favourite word, to saying those very same words. It is in the early days, when speech is still immature, that signing will continue to enhance and facilitate communication. Then, when it is no longer needed, it automatically falls away.

One way to continue to encourage this development is by beginning to give your child more choices. In the early stages, a generic sign for 'eat' was entirely appropriate for whatever food your baby liked. Now choices of favourite foods and drinks will be fun for your baby and for you. Would you like milk? Or maybe water? Which would you like: apple or banana? Baked beans or toast? Try using some of the signs provided below and on the accompanying CD-ROM to help you with some preferred foods. If you don't know, and you can't find the signs for your baby's favourite foods, then be prepared to be inventive and consistent with the signs you invent. Keep in mind that baby signing is a superb tool to help you and your baby understand and enjoy each other even more.

WHICH

How to sign it
Start as if you are signing 'aeroplane' (make a fist, palm down and thumb and little finger sticking out) use thumb and forefinger to 'seesaw between the choices'.

When to use it
As the action suggests, this is a great one to use when offering your child a choice – maybe he can't make up his mind which item of clothing to wear, or which piece of fruit to choose. Use this sign when you are asking '*Which* one would you like?'

Insight

Obviously the older your child gets, the more appropriate it is to begin giving choices. When you do offer a choice, try to keep it to a limit of two things. It can be easy to overwhelm a child with too many choices.

Many of the early choices we give our children begin with the variety of food we offer them. For some parents feed time can become a bit of a battleground. Offering a choice between two foods can help alleviate this and help the move towards a peaceful mealtime. Below are a few food choices you may wish to implement with your child.

APPLE

How to sign it
Mime eating an apple.

BANANA

How to sign it
Mime opening a banana.

TOAST

How to sign it
Fingers together, palms facing you, pop both hands up as if they are toast popping out of the toaster.

CAKE

How to sign it
One hand flat, palm down, the other hand (clawed) comes down on top, remaining clawed.

Figure 7.1 Cake.

How to sign it
One arm flat against your body, with hand up by opposite shoulder.
With the other hand (fingers together), tap the elbow twice.

Figure 7.2 Biscuit.

Speech sounds

In order to speak clearly, babies need to master a wide range of speech sounds – vowels, diphthongs and consonants. It is suggested that the signs help to differentiate speech sounds for babies and children, whose articulation can then improve considerably.
So playing around with fun sounds can be a wonderful way to encourage the practice and awareness of the different sounds we use in speech. There are many of them to master and some children can take a long time to say some of these sounds correctly.

Insight
To help your child with speech sounds, play a game pulling various toys out of a bag – almost overemphasize the sound the toy or animal makes, for example 'mooooo' for cow, 'neeeeowwww' for an airplane.

Use every opportunity to show your baby how to enjoy simple speech sounds and be assured that there is nothing wrong if, for the time being, your baby calls a clock a 'tick-tock', an ambulance a 'nee-naw' or a sheep a 'baa-baa'. Ideally you should repeat, 'yes a nee-naw, that's an ambulance, isn't it?' Anything that encourages vocalisation and enjoyment of communication is definitely a good thing!

A sign can be held static as a model to imitate. Hands can be moulded and shaped into signs far more easily than sounds can be shaped into words. (Grove 1986)

Sometimes babies charmingly and spontaneously use signs in combination, as their expressive capabilities are way ahead of their verbal skills. It is common for first-rate little signers to sign 'Where Daddy?' or 'Dog gone'. By giving babies an opportunity to 'name' objects at a very young age using signs, they soon have the ability to form such simple sentences. This often begins by using just signs, but may progress to a combination of signs and words. Therein lies the temptation for you to begin signing longer sentences, using a few signs each time. However, baby signing does not intend to keep up with your baby in this explosion of grammatical achievement (unless, of course, you are signing action songs or are keen for your baby to become bilingual in BSL, in which case you should enrol on an accredited course). Typically, developing babies do not need to be shown signs in combination, or in fuller sentences. Everyday speech has a rhythm and a natural lilt. It is important for babies to pick up on this, as they are beginning to form small immature sentences of their own. It is amazing to think our pre-verbal babies can communicate in sentences. Below, Jo tells how her daughter uses a combination of signs to communicate before speech.

My daughter Jess is now 15 months old and signing in sentences. 'More' is her favourite sign, and very well used – 'more swing', 'more banana', 'more music', 'more swimming', 'more, more, more'! But she also has a great range of signs. Speech that cannot yet be clearly understood is made clearer by use of the appropriate sign at the same time, so the confusion

between her desire to see 'Nana' and to eat a 'banana' is
becoming less frequent!

Jo and Jess from Bristol

**REMEMBER: Even if your child begins signing fuller sentences,
you should still keep your signing simple and offer only one sign
per sentence (unless, of course, you are signing action songs).**

Reading a book together

It is never too early to read with your child – in fact, many libraries
will actively encourage parents to sign up very young babies and use
the vast resources they have on offer. Some of the best opportunities to
enjoy signing with your baby come when you look at a book together.
There are so many colourful books for babies, full of pictures that
show everyday objects such as animals, vehicles, food, routines – lots
to talk about, and objects that your baby may well know the sign for.

When your baby already knows and uses a few signs, you can both
enjoy a book together, naming the pictures you see with the signs
you know. From your baby's point of view, books become more
of a shared experience, so rather than always being read to, your
child has a wonderful opportunity to 'read' some pages to you.
Many signing babies love to 'read' straight through picture books,
offering a sign for everything they see – they find it great fun.

WORD OF CAUTION...

Obviously there are great benefits to introducing books early to
your child. However, please be aware it is not the most ideal way
for your baby to learn new signs. This is primarily because you are
both enjoying looking at the pages rather than each other. This is
why this topic has been included with signing with older toddlers
and children, rather than earlier on in this book. On the other
hand, your baby is highly likely to be off to a great start with a
love of books if they are already a strong little signer.

Again it's important to remember the golden rules of baby signing: be relaxed and avoid getting your baby to 'perform'. So don't put any pressure on your baby to sign words just because you know he can, as there will undoubtedly be times when your baby will want you to do all the work.

Phonics

You may think your 16-month-old baby is too young for the alphabet, but you may be surprised to learn that your baby already has some building blocks in place for learning to read. Think about what your baby already understands so far about language – that words and signs are symbolic of individual things that they see, want and think about. This is now natural for them and being taken for granted. In the next few years the process will begin of recognizing different symbols on a page to represent these words.

Rather than teach the alphabet as 'ay, bee, see, dee' it is more helpful to use what is known as the phonetic sounds – 'ahh, buh, cuh, duh'. This can help children identify initial letters of familiar words as they begin to come phonetically aware. It is important to pronounce the letters correctly so your baby knows how they actually sound in words. Some of them are voiced, for example 'b' would be pronounced 'buh' and 'd' would be pronounced 'duh', whereas 'f' and 'h' would be unvoiced, for example they would be the whispered consonants 'ffff' and 'huh'.

Insight
As your child becomes more proficient in his signing, this is a great opportunity to begin to play phonic games with. For example, when he is clearly saying or signing the word 'ball' you can begin saying and signing the first letter of a word instead of signing the actual word.

You will find early alphabet books are a great resource for learning phonics. If your child is competent in signing certain words consistently and/or is trying to say those same words, this is an opportune time to begin introducing first letter sounds. By showing your child a sign for a letter sound, the visual clue can help him remember and identify it. This is the same as when he learnt the early gestures ('eat', 'drink', 'milk', 'more'). Your baby's brain will store the visual image of the sign along with the sound of the word – which in turn facilitates word retrieval and builds vocabulary. Using letter signs can build on understanding and awareness of individual phonemes, a major step towards reading and spelling.

I began signing with my daughter Amy when she was six weeks old. I had intended to start when she was born but just couldn't get my head together enough at first! She did her first sign at 11 months and had 25 signs before she said a word at 13 months. She is now just two years old and I still find signing such a help! Amy has more language than any of her peers and uses full sentences with tenses and pronouns. We are now working on her letters and being able to sign the sounds as well as say them has really helped. We have always signed people's names using the first letter and Amy began to make links between them herself by saying 'B...Becky, like B...Brian'. Now Amy can readily identify what sound any word begins with, and can sign and point to most letters of the alphabet. Signing has also really helped build Amy's confidence as she can communicate harder words to me that she can't pronounce very well. If she doesn't know the actual sign, then she will sign the first letter to cue me in and I can guess more easily! I firmly believe this has led to a happier life for all of us as she does not become frustrated. I would definitely recommend signing for all ages as I believe that anything that enhances communication can only be a good thing!

Zoe Desmier

Insight

There is no set age or rush to introduce concepts such as the alphabet. Many parents have found it becomes a natural progression once a child has mastered one activity or, as

(Contd)

in this case, becomes more proficient in signing. Parents recognize when their child is ready to move on to another concept, such as learning individual letters.

At the time you are introducing phonics and first letter sounds to your child, you may find some of your story reading changes. Imagine your child has just seen a bird on the page and signed (and maybe tried to say) 'bird', as this is a word and sign he is familiar with. Your conversation may go something like this: 'Yes that's right, it's a bird. Bird starts with the letter "buh"' (signing the letter B). You may find your child begins to mimic your sign as well as the sounds.

The car is another great place for learning new words and letter sounds. Even as your child progresses towards speech, or indeed is proficient in speech, you may find on any given journey he will enjoy pointing out the many things he sees – a train, a motorbike, a tree, etc. You can confirm his effort, congratulating him on correct recognition, and use the opportunity to tell him that train begins with the letter 't'. This is such a straightforward way to introduce him to the concepts of reading and spelling. This game can progress from what a particular word starts with, to what it ends with, and then later, all the letters in between!

Insight

Signing continued on for our family during the process of learning to read. One child in particular would give up very quickly if he was unable easily to recognize a new word. A signing prompt was a great encouragement for him.

Parents of signing babies have commented on how observant they tend to be, growing into confident children who develop impressive memories, enabling them to concentrate better on set tasks. These are often the crucial skills for starting the process of reading. Alongside that, signing babies often have improved fine motor skills and dexterity as a result of signing, which can only pave the way in assisting with pencil control and writing skills later on.

Colours

For older babies who are used to grasping new words and concepts with accompanying gestures, the signs for colours can be fun and a terrific memory aid. Begin by pointing out the primary colours: red, yellow and blue. As Helen and Eloise discovered, beginning the day with deciding what colour to wear is a great way to introduce these simple signs.

Eloise has continued to sign although she has dropped her favourites – the animals (with the exception of 'penguin') – and has picked up on colours instead. We've had several signing conversations about what colour clothes she will wear and often she is insistent it has to be either pink or blue.

Helen Tillinghast

Insight
The signs for 'cat', 'eat' and 'train' can easily be remembered as they mimic a particular activity or object. Colours are slightly different in this regard, and therefore can sometimes be a little harder to remember. Under most of the colours I have added a tip to help you remember the relevant colour sign.

RED

How to sign it
Use the tip of your index finger to move across your lower lip.

Tip: Think of putting red lipstick on with your finger.

BLUE

How to sign it
Run your right index finger along the back of your left hand.

Tip: Think of running your finger along your blue vein.

YELLOW

How to sign it
Hold your left hand up with palm facing out, fingers together, thumb apart. With the index finger of your other hand, touch the outside join of your left thumb and index finger twice.

Tip: Not only are you making a 'Y', this is actually the sign for the letter Y.

GREEN

How to sign it
Hold one hand still, palm down, then with the other hand flat, palm up, move it over the back of the still hand.

Figure 7.3 Green.

Tip: Do this as if scything grass.

Now our little boy is beginning to talk we are still finding signing useful, in fact, possibly even more so. He is learning his colours and, because he can sign as he speaks, we can tell, for example, whether he is saying 'yellow' (which otherwise sounds a lot like 'hello'), 'red' or 'green' (which sound the same when he says the words). I'm convinced signing has helped his vocabulary; at the very least it has reassured me that he understands words and recognizes pictures, because he has been able to sign his recognition (e.g. when we read a book together, or seeing birds and animals in the garden or the park) for many months before he began to speak.

Jane Kirkby and Ben

ORANGE

How to sign it
Hold an open hand at the side of your mouth, and then close it tight.

Tip: Do this as if squeezing an orange with your hand.

PINK

How to sign it
Touch your cheek with the tip of your index finger, making a small stroke.

Tip: Think of applying blusher with your finger.

PURPLE

How to sign it
Make an 'O' shape with your index finger and thumb. Brush this twice across the tip of the other index finger.

Tip: Think of miming the letter 'P'.

WHITE

How to sign it
Mime picking at your collar.

Tip: Think of white-collar worker!

BROWN

How to sign it
*With a flat hand, make small circles on the inside of the
opposite wrist.*

BLACK

How to sign it
With an inward-facing fist, make a small circle on your cheek.

Weather

Talking about the weather may be a national pastime, but it
provides you with a daily opportunity to introduce your child to
new signs and a fresh understanding of the world around him. And
it's fun when your baby is enjoying these things. Snow is a glorious
wonder that many children will get excited about when they see and
feel it for the first time; fog, wind and rain mean wellington boots
and puddles – plenty for you to talk and sing about.

Weather signs can be incorporated into routines, and used when
you are talking about going out – 'We need to put our coat on
because it's *raining*', or 'It's *sunny* today, we are going to wear our
hats and go to the park.' These signs also go hand in hand with the
'hot' and 'cold' signs, which can be found on pages 85 and 87.

RAIN

How to sign it
Wiggling fingers mime rainfall – start high and come down.

SUN

How to sign it
Make a circle shape in the air.

SNOW

How to sign it
Like rain, but with your hands swirling down in front of your face.

WINDY

How to sign it
With palms facing you, 'fan' hands in front of your face.

As you may well have noticed, unlike the colour signs, the weather signs are mimicking the meaning of the word – like 'making pictures in the air', so they are much easier to remember. Also bear in mind, it isn't always necessary to show your child the 'perfect' sign, demonstrated without flaw, but more important that you continue to communicate, to show him signs for the world about him, and to be consistent with any sign that you choose – even if you make one up yourself!

Potty/toilet-training

In Chapter 3 we briefly covered the 'clean' and 'dirty' signs and looked at how we can use them as a prelude to potty training. Some parents choose to begin training their child within a few weeks of birth and others start putting their child on the potty once he can sit up unaided, between six and nine months of age. We have included potty-training signs within the chapter on signing with older children, as the majority of parents in the Western world wait until their toddler is ready, which can be as early as 18 months and up to around three years old.

Insight
I realized (with my third child!) that around 20 minutes after eating she was scrunching up her face and filling her nappy. I began to sign 'toilet' to her, knowing at some point in the future she would make the connection. After a few days
(Contd)

I wondered why I was signing and watching her fill her nappy – I might as well put her on the toilet or potty! After just a few times of putting her on, she was doing a wee and poo in the potty. Obviously at six months of age she isn't toilet-trained, it's more 'toilet timing' at the moment, but it is something I hadn't considered with my two boys. I am confident however that she will be toilet-trained much earlier than they were. I've also discovered that 50 per cent of babies are toilet-trained by the time they are one – not something we often see in Western society, especially since disposable nappies are commonplace.

Whatever your method of toilet-training, you will find the following signs beneficial.

TOILET

How to sign it
The middle finger crosses your body to make two small upward brushes high on the opposite collarbone.

Figure 7.4 Toilet/potty.

When to use it

This sign can be used to indicate that your child needs to go to the toilet, so therefore can be applied whether they use the toilet or potty. Some parents use this sign when they know their child is filling his nappy from a young age; some begin to use it in the months leading up to, and during potty training; others continue to use it long after their child has got speech. It is such a useful sign to either tell or ask your child if he needs to use the toilet.

Insight

I'm not sure at what age you stop asking or reminding your child to use the toilet. This is a sign that is still in regular use in our family, long after I thought my signing days were over! It is far less embarrassing for an eight-year-old if mum discreetly signs 'toilet' when she notices the 'toilet jiggle' rather than asking him if he needs to go in front of his peers!

POTTY

Although you may wish to use the toilet sign for the toilet or the potty, this sign is an alternative potty sign, which can be used should you wish to distinguish between the two.

How to sign it
With hands shoulder-width apart, mime putting a potty from one side to in front of you.

DRY

How to sign it
With one hand, fingers in towards your palm, your thumb rubs over the nails of the other fingers (little finger first).

WET

How to sign it
Fingertips touch your lip and rub together (miming showing they have become 'wet').

Figure 7.5 Wet.

SIT

How to sign it
Two flat hands, one on top of the other, move down once, miming sitting.

Figure 7.6 Sit.

When should you stop signing?

This is a very common question. Some people, having begun to learn a new way of communicating with their baby, are less than keen to drop the signs completely. This may well be true if you have a deaf friend or relative you wish to communicate more effectively with. Alternatively, you may have discovered that even simple signing with your child can be a great asset to further developing your relationship, simultaneously enhancing his learning and communication development. Many playgroups, schools and even churches will now use some form of Makaton or other speech-supported signing system to reinforce audible commands, songs or familiar routines. Children learn best when more than one sense (visual, auditory, sensory) is stimulated, as we touched upon in Chapter 5. Older children who have difficulty with spellings, or a list of facts to remember, will often find signing can add that extra dimension to their learning and help reinforce what they are trying to learn. Families of children with ADHD and learning difficulties will often incorporate movement with learning as they know this can aid memory retention.

Parents have found it can become second nature to 'talk' with their hands as well as their voice. A major benefit to parents is the way they can communicate with their child in crowded places, or to bring particular emphasis to something without raising their voice. The most obvious example is catching one of your children jigging up and down, engrossed in something else – all you need to do is call their name, sign 'toilet' and 'now' and off he trots, accident avoided as well as any embarrassment in front of his friends. Another sign you may notice parents using in the park is the 'dangerous' sign. This is particularly useful if you are occupied with one child, and notice the other child somewhere where he shouldn't be. Again, calling his name and using the 'no' and 'dangerous' sign can be all that is required.

I have watched pre-schoolers using signs to emphasize a point, especially if they really want that second biscuit. It's amazing how often the word 'please' will be further reinforced with the accompanying sign!

So don't feel just because your child has started speaking, and is making great strides in this area, that your hands need to stop 'talking' so much. You and your child will still get a lot of benefit and probably enjoy the process too.

Children with sign language skills are bringing something valuable and worthwhile into their community, as well as gaining the advantage of a second language. If you have enjoyed signing with your baby, maybe this will inspire you to learn BSL... you never know!

TEST YOUR KNOWLEDGE

1 *What role does signing play in emerging speech, some of which will not yet be intelligible?*

2 *What is the average age at which a baby says his first word?*

3 *What is the average age when more rapid speech growth tends to happen in toddlers?*

4 *As toddlers begin to use more words, what is the impact on their signing?*

5 *What do children need to master a wide range of in order to speak clearly?*

6 *Why is it important not to sign fuller sentences, or to use signs in combination as your child develops in his signing and speech?*

7 *How would you judge that your child was ready to move from signing words, to signing the beginning letter of a word?*

8 *In what creative ways can you assist your child to learn individual letters of the alphabet?*

9 *In what ways can signing benefit an older child?*

10 *When is an appropriate age to stop signing?*

See answer section at the back of the book.

8

Frequently asked questions

In this chapter you will learn:
- *answers to the most common questions asked of signing teachers*
- *what to do if you are worried about your child's speech development*
- *differences between various signing systems*
- *ways to learn through Sing and Sign.*

If my baby learns signs will she still learn to talk?

This has got to be the most common question that is asked. Yes, of course she will! Signs are never used *instead* of words and therefore your baby will be greatly encouraged to communicate verbally, and in no way discouraged. Baby signing is not a replacement for talking to your baby, in practice it encourages you to talk *more*! The use of gesture is a natural form of early communication and won't hinder the process of learning to talk – in fact it actually gives it a boost!

'Bye-bye' is often among the earliest words babies say. Think about how we all encourage babies to wave 'goodbye', recognizing they will enjoy this as well as helping to make them aware of an important concept. There seem to be four typical stages to this process:

1 *Your baby will first start to recognize and enjoy Mummy and Daddy waving goodbye.*

2   *Your baby will start to imitate you when you wave (probably to great applause and family excitement!).*
3   *Your baby will start to wave spontaneously as you get ready to leave (this is when we would say the baby is 'signing').*
4   *Your baby will say the words 'bye-bye!', while waving.*

The waving has actually encouraged this baby to say the word because of the positive feedback and enjoyment of the sign. It is the same principle with other words and signs.

Insight
The 'bye-bye' illustration is actually very useful to use with family and friends that are unfamiliar with signing. It is a natural sign that most babies will use and clearly shows that it doesn't inhibit speech.

What happens to signs as a baby begins to speak?

Babies may use signs and immature speech together for a while. As speech improves, even the most enthusiastic little signers will start to drop their signs in favour of spoken words until they are no longer used. A toddler's immature speech will soon bloom into two- and three-word spoken combinations and overtake their single-word signing prowess.

There is much variation among babies in how they start to talk, and signing babies are no different. Some babies' first words are their signing words, such as 'more', 'all gone', or 'car'. This is probably because they have heard these words over and over and are used to communicating them. Speaking them is the obvious next step.

If your baby begins to say some words while simultaneously using the sign, it is entirely appropriate for you to stop using these signs. It is worthwhile continuing with signing for longer, more complex words that may be hard for a young child to say, as well as introducing the alphabet with sign. Signing can continue to give you the opportunity to communicate effectively even when speech is fairly fluent.

Insight

I can remember a time when my almost two-year-old was asking where the **$@!* was. Despite repeated efforts at trying to understand him, I eventually said 'Sign it for mummy'. He then signed 'hippopotamus' (a huge mouthful for any young child – it was no wonder I couldn't understand his attempt). Hippo was a very recent acquisition, and I was so pleased I had given him a sign for it as I was unfamiliar with his attempt at saying the word.

Sometimes a baby's first words may be those they do not yet sign, or do not know the sign for – there seems to be no hard or fast rule. You may even find that your baby has some favourite signs that they will continue to use for a while, even though they can say many other more complex words. For my son, 'sorry' was one of those words that remained signed for a very long time in favour of being spoken. However, this is a word that even some adults find hard to say! Sometimes when babies have all but finished with their signs, they revert to using them when they are upset or tired, using the old gestures as a way of emphasizing what they are trying to say – shouting in sign!

Why is my baby taking a while to use signs?

This is not unusual – consistency at home is usually the key but some babies are just later to communicate than others. Put no pressure on yourself or your baby. Your baby's desire to communicate with you will be strong and your patience will be rewarded. If your baby is taking a while to use signs, it really is worth persevering. Remember, your baby is benefiting so much from your signing input, and will sign when she has something to say. The key is to watch what your baby is interested in, for my first son it was animals (and still is!). Try not to emphasize 'parent-pleasing' signs initially, such as 'please' and 'thank you', but rather watch what it is your baby is looking at, as these motivational signs are the ones that bring most success. If you feel impatient that your baby has not yet returned the signs you have been using, don't worry, and remember the journey towards speech is not a race. The joy and excitement of your child's first sign will make your patience worthwhile – I promise!

Could signing inhibit a baby's natural instinct to learn to talk?

You can reassure all who ask this common question that baby signing is beneficial to speech development. As we have already established, it is vital always to say the word as it is signed. In this way, you support and emphasize the spoken label and the sign is not a replacement for it. The use of gesture is a natural stage of early communication and the introduction of baby signing will inspire a baby to develop enhanced communication skills and will greatly expand her vocabulary.

Unfortunately, some people are of the erroneous opinion that frustration at being unable to communicate adequately is 'good for' babies and that it creates the urge to speak. This is a myth.

Insight
Extensive research has shown that children become better communicators when their early attempts at communication are understood and responded to, not when they are frustrated at not being understood.

Marilyn Daniels PhD (Associate Professor of Speech Communication at Pennsylvania State University) says:

Including sign language in the communication mix can eliminate the frustration both parent and child often experience as they attempt to comprehend each other. It fosters pleasant discourse, clarifies meaning and creates better understanding between them. With the keener understanding, there also comes an authentic grasp of content. Sign does not hinder language development in any way, rather it fosters it. It picks up on the natural visual acuity young children possess and uses it to the child's advantage.

How can I encourage my child to sign to me more?

Although we have encouraged you to start with simple signs such as 'eat', 'drink', and 'milk', this can be more for your benefit to enable you to get into the habit of signing to your baby, as they are early signs that you can use many times during the day. However, these are not always the first signs babies will use – maybe because we are generally good parents who know when our child is hungry or thirsty the majority of the time, or they are just offered it many times a day and therefore do not need to ask for it. Asking your child more open-ended questions using the 'what' sign (waggling your index finger from side to side) is really useful. Giving her a choice of toy for example – '*What* do you want? Bird or duck?' Or even something as simple as '*What* do you want? Play or food?' To begin with she may point and grab at the item she wants, but consistently showing her the correct sign will reap you the rewards.

In Sing and Sign class an early sign for many of the babies is the 'where' sign. This is primarily because we have a wonderful surprise box in which our Jessie Cat hides. We begin singing 'Where oh where oh where is Jessie?' The squeals of delight as once again Jessie pops out are just magical! However, it is a great motivational sign, and one that children seem to pick up very easily. Don't forget, babies will sign what is important to them.

What should I do if I am worried about my child's speech?

Babies are different and there is wide variation in how babies develop their speech and language skills, just as there is when children learn to walk. However, certain milestones are typical, so if you are at all concerned about any aspect of your baby's speech or communication, talk it through with your health visitor or doctor, who can refer your child to a speech and language therapist for advice. You can also make this referral yourself if necessary. Details of local speech and language therapy services can be found through the telephone directory, GP clinic or the library.

What are the different signing systems?

There are two main signing systems in the UK: British Sign Language (BSL) and Makaton (or systems based upon this).

BSL is a language in its own right, and is the main means of communication within the deaf community, who are passionate about their language. When signing with BSL you often won't sign fluently because the language has its own grammar. For example, if you want to say 'What is your name?' when using BSL you would sign, 'Name, you what?' There are some baby-signing programmes within the UK that use BSL. It is very important to respect BSL as a separate language and if you wish to learn it, or intend to teach your baby to sign as a second language, it is essential to do so properly on an accredited course (Council for the Advancement of Communication with Deaf People, CACDP).

Makaton and other systems such as Signalong are 'sign supporting systems' which use signs or gestures to support speech; they are not an additional language like BSL. Makaton and Signalong are widely used in nurseries and schools with children who need help with communication. The signs are compatible with many in BSL, but the approach is distinct as signs are only used to highlight key spoken words. The main aim when signing with your baby is to encourage speech, and not to teach an alternative language.

Sing and Sign is based on widely used UK gesture systems such as Makaton, Say It and Sign It, Signalong and others based on BSL. These systems are designed for use *with* speech and are used by speech and language professionals, as well as in nurseries and schools.

For parents who are already using different signs, it doesn't matter which signs you use (for example, many parents have seen the sign for 'more' in American Sign Language on TV and have adopted that). It is the philosophy and approach that count. If your baby has already become familiar with certain signs, you do not need to alter them just to fit in with a different approach.

Insight

I do, however, know of many families who have chosen to switch to the UK version of signs, and their children have adapted very well. Whether to make the switch or stay with what you have begun is a matter of personal preference, but once you decide it's important to remain consistent.

Help! I don't know the sign for...

Often when parents have started classes and are seeing the benefits of signing, they want to begin signing everything – from every toy, to every type of food. Remember, in the early stages, the key is simplicity. We would therefore recommend using the sign for 'eat' (using one hand, bunch your fingers together and tap a few times to your lips – saying the word 'eat') for breakfast, dinner, lunch etc., and not necessarily trying to sign, peas, potato or butternut squash! 'Eat/food' is sufficient in the early stages with your baby. It is only with the older baby or toddler that we would recommend giving many more choices with different food types. You will therefore notice a lot more variety in the Sing and Sign Stage 2 DVD and classes.

It isn't always important to sign the correct sign for a particular item – if you don't know it, and it isn't on the CD-ROM accompanying this book, then you may wish to be inventive. Being consistent with a sign is just as beneficial as using the correct sign. The list provided isn't exhaustive, but should offer you an excellent starting place.

Another benefit of signing for us is that because signing now comes so naturally to him, Ben makes up his own signs to communicate things that he can't manage to say. So far, he has 'invented' signs for glasses/spectacles, watering can, colouring and 'Bob the Builder'! It is this proactivity in communication which is, for me, one of the most valuable benefits of signing.

Jane Kirby

How can I learn the Sing and Sign way?

Sign with Your Baby is based on the Sing and Sign method of baby signing, and references within the book have indicated a variety of aspects to the programme. Below is a brief overview. For further information please go to www.singandsign.com.

In a class: You can attend a weekly Sing and Sign group with other parents and babies. These fun music groups are run across the country.

At home: The Sing and Sign DVD contains signed action songs and nursery rhymes. Sing and Sign is suitable for babies from six months, while 'More Sing and Sign' is suitable for toddlers aged over 14 months.

Online: The Sign and Sign website provides access to the extensive members' dictionary of baby signs for parents who want to create their baby's own personalized signing resource. Also available is a baby-signing discussion forum where you can share stories and get advice from teachers, experts and other parents.

> **Insight**
>
> Create and print out your own personalized signing resource to share with family, friends or others who look after your baby when you can't be there. It can also be useful to print out certain signs to use as reminders around the house.

TEST YOUR KNOWLEDGE

1 Why will signing not inhibit your child's ability to talk?

2 What happens to children's signing repertoire as they begin to speak fluently?

3 Why can it be useful to continue signing as speech develops?

4 What might cause children to return to certain signs once they have moved on from signing?

5 What is the main thing to remember if your child is taking a while to sign?

6 When will your baby begin to sign?

7 What signs might be described as 'parent-pleasing'?

8 What is the main difference between BSL and Makaton?

9 If you have already taught your baby a few signs that are different from those shown in this book, what should your approach be?

10 What should you do if you can't find the sign for an important word you use regularly?

See answer section at the back of the book.

Signing dictionary

Below is a quick reference guide for all the signs covered in *Sign with Your Baby*. Many of these signs can also be found on the accompanying CD-ROM. Those marked with an asterisk (*) are ones that are illustrated in the book.

AEROPLANE – PAGE 82
Make a fist and then have your thumb and little finger sticking out as if they are wings. You can then move your 'plane' through the sky, making the appropriate 'neeeooooowwww' sound!

ALL GONE/FINISHED – PAGE 38*
Begin by holding your fists together with your palms facing inwards, then move your hands out so your hands are flat and facing down.

ANGRY – PAGE 99*
Clawed hands, with palms facing you, make small movements alternating up and down.

ANIMALS – PAGE 77
With palms facing down, mime 'prowling' hands going forward.

APPLE – PAGE 160
Mime eating an apple.

AUNTIE – PAGE 120
With index and middle finger bent and slightly apart, tap your chin.

BANANA – PAGE 160

Mime opening a banana.

BATH – PAGE 70*

Cross your arms over your chest and mime washing yourself.

BED – PAGE 73

Put your hands together on one side of your face, and then tilt your head – as if your hands are becoming your pillow.

BEE – PAGE 79

With your thumb and index finger together, make random loops in the air. Great with a good 'bzzzzzzz' sound too!

BIRD – PAGE 79

With your thumb and index finger of one hand, open and close several times (keep the other three fingers clenched) – as if you are doing a mime for opening and closing a bird's beak.

BISCUIT – PAGE 161*

One arm flat against your body, with hand up by opposite shoulder. With the other hand (fingers together), tap the elbow twice.

BLACK – PAGE 170

With an inward-facing fist, make a small circle on your cheek.

BLUE – PAGE 167

Run your right index finger along the back of your left hand.

BOAT – PAGE 82*

Touch your fingertips together, palms facing inwards but apart, so you are making a boat's 'bow' shape. Move your boat shape forward.

BOOK – PAGE 73

With both hands clasped together, mime opening a book.

BOY – PAGE 118

Index finger sweeps under your chin from left to right.

BROTHER – PAGE 118*

Make a fist, with thumbs up, knuckles inwards, and rub up and down.

BROWN – PAGE 170

With a flat hand, make small circles on the inside of the opposite wrist.

BUGGY – PAGE 62

Mime pushing a buggy in front of you.

BUS – PAGE 62

With arms parallel to your shoulders and straight arms, mime a big steering wheel.

CAKE – PAGE 160*

One hand flat, palm down, the other hand (clawed) comes down on top, remaining clawed.

CAR – PAGES 62 AND 82
With hands in front of you and bent arms, mime a small steering wheel.

CAREFUL – PAGE 92*
With your thumb and index finger form the letter 'C'. Move two 'C' shaped hands down and out from your eyes.

CAT – PAGE 77*
With both hands making 'V' shapes with first two fingers, mime whiskers coming out from your nose.

CHANGE (NAPPY) – PAGE 66*
Hold your fists together and twist from side to side.

CHICKEN – PAGE 80
Your elbows become wings, so move them in and out, like a chicken.

CLEAN – PAGE 68*
Sweep one palm across the other upturned palm.

COAT – PAGE 61
Mime pulling a coat around your shoulders.

COLD – PAGE 87
Clench your fists directly in front of your chest, then in small movements shake them up and down, as if you were miming a 'brrrr!'

COUSIN – PAGE 120
Make a 'C' shape with your thumb and forefinger, and brush this twice under your chin.

CROCODILE – PAGE 79
Think of your hands and arms as the jaws of a croc, so with both hands mime a big snapping action.

DADDY – PAGE 117
With closed index and middle finger tap twice on the closed index and middle finger of the opposite hand.

DANGEROUS – PAGE 84*
Start with your index finger touching between your eyes. Use a straight hand, facing sideways and move down strongly in an arc.

DIRTY – PAGE 68
Rub inside of wrists together, as if you have dirty cuffs.

DOCTOR – PAGE 107
With thumb and index finger, place on edge of wrist (as if taking a pulse).

DOG – PAGE 78*
Index and third fingers of both hands move down once in front of your chest.

DOLL – PAGE 74*
Hands in rocking position, but held still.

DRINK – PAGE 35*
Shape your hand as if you were holding a beaker and lift it a few times to your mouth.

DRY – PAGE 173
With one hand, fingers in towards your palm, your thumb rubs over nails of the other fingers (little finger first).

DUCK – PAGE 79
Open and close your whole hand as if it were a beak making a 'quacking' move.

EAT – PAGE 32*
Bunch your fingertips together and gently tap the corner of your mouth.

ELEPHANT – PAGE 79
Make a fist, take it up to your nose and mime a big trunk, with a little flourish at the end.

FARM – PAGE 59
Think of a farmer wearing braces. With both thumbs mime pulling braces forward.

FINISHED/ALL GONE – PAGE 38*
Begin by holding your fists together with your palms facing inwards, then move your hands out so your hands are flat and facing down.

FISH – PAGE 78*
With your hand facing sideways, mime a fish tail in a 'swimming' motion.

FRIEND – PAGE 121*
Clasp one hand with the other – as if shaking hands – mime this up and down.

FRIGHTENED – PAGE 98
Clawed hand trembles in front of your chest.

FUNNY – PAGE 98
Make a 'C' with index finger and thumb, and move up and down in front of your jaw, as if you are miming jaw moving up and down with laughter.

GENTLE – PAGE 88*
With one hand, slowly and gently stroke the back of your other hand.

GIRL – PAGE 119
Index finger makes two small strokes down from your cheek towards your mouth.

GOING OUT – PAGE 58*
Cup your hand slightly, palm facing downwards, and mime 'going over the wall'.

GRANDAD/GRANDPA, ETC. – PAGE 119*
With fingers spread apart, hand sideways, put the tip of your thumb on your forehead, and move your hand forwards and down making small arcs in front of you.

GRANDMA/GRANNY, ETC. – PAGE 120
With fingers spread, hand facing sideways, make small arc movements down from your chin.

GREEN – PAGE 168*
Hold one hand still, palm down, then with the other hand flat, palm up, move it over the back of the still hand.

HAPPY – PAGE 97*
Keep left cupped hand still, then rub right cupped hand from index finder out to thumb. Rub cupped hands with glee.

HAT – PAGE 64
With a flat hand, put a 'hat' on your head, by patting your head.

HELP – PAGE 49*
With outstretched arms, make the thumbs up sign with your right hand, put this hand on top of your upturned left palm, then move both hands together towards your chest.

HOME – PAGE 64*
Mime a roof, with straight hands and your fingertips touching.

HOT – PAGE 85*
With five fingers spread apart, quickly touch your fingers to your lips and then withdraw them.

HURRY UP – PAGE 92
Index finger quickly strikes the side of the other index finger.

HURT/PAIN – PAGE 104*
Point both index fingers towards each other and keep prodding them together.

LAUGH – PAGE 98
Make a 'C' with index finger and thumb, and move up and down in front of your jaw, as if you are miming jaw moving up and down with laughter.

LOOK – PAGE 90
Use your index finger (as if pointing to your eye) then swiftly move it away in the direction of where you are indicating to your child to look.

LOVE – PAGE 108
Two hands cross lovingly across your chest.

MEDICINE – PAGE 106*
Make a loosely held fist with your left hand, then with the little fingertip of your right hand trace around the top of the fist – as if tracing the opening of a small jar.

MILK – PAGE 36*
Make a fist, then open and close your fist as if you are milking.

MONKEY – PAGE 80
For this one, there is nothing for it but to look like a monkey, so with both arms stretched out horizontally, bend them at the elbow and start scratching under your arms!

MORE – PAGE 33*
Make a fist with one hand, and then with the other hand flat, cover it over the top of the fist, just like you are pushing a cork into a bottle.

MUMMY – PAGE 117
Index, middle and ring fingers tap twice on the opposite palm.

MUSIC (CLASS) – PAGE 59
With index fingers in the air, wave from side to side as if conducting.

MUSLIN – PAGE 75*
Make a fist, facing inwards, and rub this up and down on your cheek.

NANNA/NANNY, ETC. – PAGE 120
With fingers spread, hand facing sideways, make small arc movements down from your chin.

NAPPY CHANGE – PAGE 66*
Hold your fists together and twist from side to side.

NAUGHTY – PAGE 88
With a clenched fist in front of you, raise your little finger.

NO – PAGE 51*
Use a flat hand facing away from your body, and make one movement starting in front of your body, taking your hand out to the side.

NOW – PAGE 91*
Start with your palms facing upwards and your fingertips facing in at chest level, then make one strong movement down to waist level.

OPEN – PAGE 51
Scrunch your hand up, and with a big flourish, open your fingers out.

ORANGE – PAGE 169
Hold an open hand at the side of your mouth, and then close it tight.

PAIN/HURT – PAGE 104*
Point both index fingers together and keep prodding them together.

PARK – PAGE 59
With a flat hand facing downwards, make a wide circle from your waist.

PINK – PAGE 169
Touch your cheek with the tip of your index finger, making a small stroke.

PLAY/TOYS – PAGE 93*
With flat hands, make small upward moving circles in front of you, rotating your wrists.

PLEASE – PAGE 108*
With a flat hand on your chin, fingertips pointing up, palm towards you, move your hand out and down from your chin in a large arc.

POTTY – PAGE 173
With hands shoulder-width apart, mime putting a potty from one side to in front of you.

PURPLE – PAGE 169
Make an 'O' shape with your index finger and thumb. Brush this twice across the tip of the other index finger.

QUICK – PAGE 92
Index finger quickly strikes the side of the other index finger.

RABBIT – PAGE 80
With your index and middle fingers make 'rabbit ears' on your head, and twitch them forward slightly.

RAIN – PAGE 170
Wiggling fingers mime rainfall – start high and come down.

RED – PAGE 167
Use the tip of your index finger to move across your lower lip.

SAD – PAGE 98
Flat hand (facing sideways, fingertips up) moves down the middle of your face.

SAND – PAGE 60*
Think of rubbing flour through your fingers. Do this action while raising your hands upwards.

SHARE – PAGE 112*
Mime 'give' and 'take' with both hands, palms faced upwards.

SHEEP – PAGE 80
With your little fingers, mime curly horns coming out from your temples.

SHOES – PAGE 61*
With one hand, make a 'bridge' and mime putting a 'shoe' on the other hand.

SHOPS – PAGE 58
With two hands starting close to your chest, mime pushing a trolley, so extend and 'push' your arms in front.

SISTER – PAGE 118
Hooked index finger taps the bridge of your nose twice.

SIT – PAGE 174*
Two flat hands, one on top of the other, move down once, miming sitting.

SLIDE – PAGE 60
Flat hand mimes sliding down.

SNOW – PAGE 171
Like rain, but with your hands swirling down in front of your face.

SORRY – PAGE 111*
Make a fist, and rub a small circle in the middle of your chest.

SUN – PAGE 170
Make a circle shape in the air.

SWIMMING POOL – PAGE 59
Mime doing breaststroke.

SWINGS – PAGE 60*
Two hands mime a swing action by your sides.

TEDDY – PAGE 74*
With gently clawed hands, cross wrists across chest and tap
your shoulders – as if you are making a cuddle gesture.

TEETH (BRUSHING TEETH) – PAGE 72
Very simply, with your index finger, mime brushing your
front teeth.

THANK YOU – PAGE 110*
With a flat hand on your chin, fingertips pointing up, palm towards
you, move your fingertips out and down from your chin in a small
static movement that should finish about *10–15 cm (4–6 in)* from
your face.

TIRED – PAGES 72 AND 98
Clench your fist and rub your eye.

TOAST – PAGE 160
Fingers together, palms facing you, pop both hands up as if they
are toast popping out of the toaster.

TOILET/POTTY – PAGE 172*

The middle finger crosses your body to make two small upward brushes high on the opposite collarbone.

TOYS/PLAY – PAGE 93*

With flat hands, make small upward moving circles in front of you, rotating your wrists.

TRAIN – PAGE 81*

With arms bent and fists clenched at your sides, mime train wheels.

UNCLE – PAGE 120

Index finger brushes back of other little finger twice.

UPSTAIRS – PAGE 72

Let your first and middle fingers of one hand make a walking movement 'up' invisible stairs.

WAIT – PAGE 113*

Put both hands in front of your body, hands flat, palms outwards, then move your hands purposefully down in front of you.

WET – PAGE 174*

Fingertips touch your lip and rub together (miming showing they have become 'wet').

WHAT – PAGE 90

Wave your index finger from side to side.

WHERE – PAGE 47*
Hold your hands in front of you with palms facing upwards, making small circles.

WHICH – PAGE 159
Start as if you are signing 'areoplane' (fist, palm down and thumb and little finger sticking out) use thumb and forefinger to 'seesaw between the choices'.

WHITE – PAGE 169
Mime picking at your collar.

WINDY – PAGE 171
With palms facing you, 'fan' hands in front of your face.

YELLOW – PAGE 168
Hold your left hand up with palm facing out, fingers together, thumb apart. With the index finger of your other hand, touch the outside join of your left thumb and index finger twice.

YES – PAGE 55*
Make a fist with your right hand and 'nod' yes (from your wrist) with your hand.

Answers to Test your knowledge questions

Chapter 2

1 From around six–seven months of age.
2 This is when children become increasingly receptive to language.
3 The ten basic guidelines for successful baby signing:
   Begin with basics such as 'eat', 'drink', 'milk', 'more' and 'all gone' (finished).
   Follow your baby's lead.
   Always say the word as you sign.
   Speak slowly but naturally.
   Keep it simple.
   Happily accept any signing attempts by your baby.
   Be consistent.
   Avoid trying to get your baby to 'perform' signs.
   Be patient and relaxed about baby signing.
   Praise, praise, praise!
4 The concentrated language input sparks connections of understanding and recognition in a baby's developing brain at a very early stage.
5 Just one sign per sentence; simplicity is key.
6 When signing a rhyme or song.
7 Babies can take just a week or several months before making their first sign.
8 One reason is that your baby has just understood the concept that a word and sign mean something, and if she repeats that back to you, she may well get what she is wanting! She hasn't yet understood that everything in her world has a different label. This follows the same pattern as acquiring speech.

Another reason is because our wonderful language can be confusing. We will often say 'Do you want that toy?', 'Can you see that train?', 'Do you want that drink?' or 'That's a sheep.' Often, without realizing it, we are reinforcing the word that – our children then interpret the sign and use it for a huge variety of objects.

9 When you say the word and sign it you are giving your child verbal and visual encouragement to communicate with you. Your child will pick up the visual clue, but also clearly hear the word behind the sign.

10 Be consistent in how you show a sign, however your baby adapts it. In general, the more your baby sees you sign, or sees a particular sign, the quicker she will recognize it.

Chapter 4

1 They are a primary feature of a baby's life, and much of her world revolves around them.

2 By crying.

3 Emotions.

4 Strong emotions and understanding of needs.

5 Frustration.

6 Confidence, self-esteem and emotional development.

7 You can begin using this sign around six–seven months of age. If your child has bumped her knee, then use the sign next to their knee. Your child will soon learn how to sign which part of her body is hurt.

8 These signs can be deemed as 'parent pleasing' signs and not particularly motivating for a young baby, however continue to show your baby these signs and use them in context.

9 Most children will perceive sharing as having to surrender a favourite toy or possession.
Be proactive in teaching your child to share. Use her favourite food as an opportunity for you to 'share' with them.
Alternatively make a game of 'sharing' a favourite toy – taking turns. This gives your child this opportunity to share in a

non-threatening environment and enables you to appropriately judge the time to 'share' it back again.

10 Your child will learn that although her needs may feel immediate, she should not expect instant gratification.

Chapter 5

1 By using signs for the names of favourite friends and relatives.

2 Grandad is a thinker – so comes down from his head, Grandma is a talker – so the sign comes down from her chin!

3 If you have a lot of close family you will need to be inventive, creating gestures that indicate personal characteristics such as glasses or a beard. Maybe you have a family member who is particularly clever, the sign for which is dragging a thumb horizontally across your forehead – or you could use the sign for an initial letter of a person's name.

4 Some families are quite complex in the number of grandparents they have, so using photos to differentiate between Grandad, Grandpa and Grandpops, for example, can be a great way to help your child use the right sign for each person.

5 It helps the children anticipate what will happen next, understand boundaries, and helps promote a calm atmosphere.

6 By giving them a copy of this book with corresponding CD-ROM, printing out a page or two of your baby's favourite signs from the online dictionary on the website (www.singandsign.com) or by showing them the Sing and Sign DVD.

7 By signing with your child you are giving him the opportunity to see, hear and do. Signing can add an extra dimension to his learning.

8 Signing with a bilingual child helps the child to connect the two (or more) languages; the sign acts as an anchor. There is scientific evidence that children who are exposed to a second language from an early age not only achieve much better results in languages, but also in maths, science and music.

9 Even though multiples tend to make sounds and gestures early on to each other, they often say their first word about a month later than most single-born children. Up to half of twins who use twin talk will also have a speech and language difficulty. This is primarily due to multiples not having as many chances as single-born children to interact directly and individually with their parents.

10 When dads learn the signs, they help to provide continuity for the child and be involved in actively communicating with the child, before he is able to talk.

Chapter 6

1 Always seek the advice of a health professional.

2 Developmental Delay is usually a diagnosis made by a doctor based on strict guidelines, usually when a child does not achieve one or more of their developmental milestones at the expected time, and there is an ongoing major delay in the process.

3 Development Delay can occur in one of many areas, for example, motor, language, social or thinking skills. Global Developmental Delay implies that the child has delays in all areas of development.

4 Developmental Delay can impact on the length of time it takes a child to learn to sign. Signing can become a vital part of the learning process and enable communication when speech may still be much further away.

5 The first three to five years of a child's life are an amazing time of development and what happens during those years stays with a child for a lifetime. That's why it is so important to watch for signs of delays in development, and to get help from professionals if you suspect problems.

6 Signalong and Makaton.

7 Maybe it is helpful to consider it in another way: if your child is already having problems with speech, then how wonderful to provide her with the opportunity to be able to communicate.

8 Glue ear is a very common condition, with one in five children (especially pre-school children) suffering with glue ear.

9 Symptoms of glue ear are:
fluctuating hearing loss
brief episodes of earache, lasting two to three hours, often at night
inability to listen or pay attention
tendency to daydream
behaviour problems/tantrums
recurrent ear infections
speech problems, especially in young children, usually mild difficulty in saying some of the quiet consonant sounds and in developing use of language generally
poor balance.

10 Ways to aid communication with a child who has hearing loss:
Make sure that you have your child's attention before starting to sign or speak to her.
Maintain good eye contact and speak clearly and naturally.
Ensure only one person is speaking at a time.
Tell everyone involved with your child about your child's condition.
If your child does not understand a word or sign, try to use a different one with the same meaning.
Try to keep background noise to a minimum.
Talk a lot to your child about what you are doing, or what your child is doing or looking at.
Try to use signs and gestures with appropriate facial expressions to support what you are saying.
Make sure your child knows when there is a new topic of conversation so that she understands the context.
Be patient. Try not to get angry when your child keeps saying 'What?', 'Pardon' or 'Uhhh'.
Take extra care when out and about with your child, especially around traffic.

Chapter 7

1 Signing can be fantastic in distinguishing what your child's ambiguous sounding word actually means. It also provides an important opportunity for you to correctly reinforce the spoken word.

2 Around his first birthday.

3 Around 18 months.

4 Continually reinforcing signs with the spoken word encourages children to start vocalizing the words they have been signing, until they drop the signs altogether in favour of speech.

5 In order to speak clearly, babies need to master a wide range of speech sounds (vowels, diphthongs and consonants).

6 Everyday speech has a rhythm and a natural lilt. It is important for babies to pick up on this, as they are beginning to form small immature sentences of their own. Too many signs will begin to alter your speech.

7 When your child is comfortable and proficient signer – or indeed saying various words – beginning to introduce the initial letter of a word is the natural and logical next step.

8 By using phonic games and alphabet books.

9 Parents of signing babies have commented on how observant they tend to be, growing into confident children who develop impressive memories enabling them to concentrate better on set tasks. These are often the crucial skills for starting the process of reading. Signing babies often have improved fine motor skills and dexterity, which can only pave the way in assisting with pencil control and writing skills later on.

10 There is no set age to stop signing. Signs will naturally fall away in favour of speech, however certain signs such as 'please' and 'thank you' or even 'toilet' may remain as part of signing repertoire for many years.

Chapter 8

1 Signs are never used instead of words and therefore your baby will be greatly encouraged to communicate verbally, and in no way discouraged.

2 As speech improves, even the most enthusiastic little signers will start to drop their signs in favour of spoken words until they are no longer used.

3 Signing can continue to give you the opportunity to communicate effectively even when speech is fairly fluent.

4 Sometimes when babies have all but finished with their signs, they revert to using them when they are upset or tired, using the old gestures as a way of emphasizing what they are trying to say – shouting in sign!

5 Your baby is benefiting so much from your signing input, and will sign when she has something to say. The key is to watch what your baby is interested in.

6 When your baby has something to 'say'.

7 Many of the 'manners' signs, particularly 'please' and 'thank you'.

8 BSL is a language in its own right, and is the main means of communication within the deaf community. When signing with BSL you often won't sign fluently because the language has its own grammar. Makaton and other systems such as Signalong use signs or gestures to support speech only.

9 For parents who are already using different signs, it doesn't matter which signs you use: it is the philosophy and approach that counts.

10 It isn't always important to sign the correct sign for a particular item – if you don't know it, and it isn't on the CD-ROM accompanying this book, then you may wish to be inventive. Being consistent with a sign is just as beneficial as using the correct sign.

Index

Headings in italics indicate signs.

....

Image credits